NEW REFORMATION SERIES

The Christian Situation Today

NORMAN PITTENGER

D1312865

LONDON
EPWORTH PRESS

© Norman Pittenger 1969

First published in 1969
by Epworth Press

Printed and bound by
The Garden City Press Limited
Letchworth, Hertfordshire

SBN 7162 0106 2

The New Reformation Series

THE past few years have seen a theological ferment which some think could herald a new Reformation. Whether it will do so is impossible to tell; in any case it is dangerous to draw historical parallels.

Yet over the last two centuries there has been a new Renaissance, a cultural revolution, which dwarfs the old. And the danger is that, in all the excitement and our desire to do something, we may be influenced more by the fashions of the age than by fidelity to truth. Christians may be tempted to count the advance of the Gospel in headlines rather than in men and women set free for living, and to substitute journalism and TV debate for the exploration of ultimate questions in the light of the new knowledge we have gained.

At the same time, theology must not be confined to the schools, and there is no more satisfactory feature of the present situation than the interchange between professionals and non-experts which paperback publishing has facilitated. After all, it is often the man or woman in the street, the office, the factory, or the laboratory who asks the questions. The attempts to answer must not be whispered in the polysyllables of common rooms or the jargon of seminars.

It is the aim of this series to dig deep into the foundations both of Christianity and of life, and to bring what is discovered to the surface in a form which can be seen clearly and understood by anyone who is sensitive to the problems of our time and is willing to exercise his mind on them and on the possibility that the Christian tradition has something relevant to say. The books will not be too lengthy and they will avoid footnotes, critical apparatus and too much technicality. The authors have been chosen because they are scholars and experts in the subjects assigned to them, but also because they are alive to the contemporary world and concerned about communication.

The method will be to look for truth about the nature of the universe and of human life and personality by seeking a fruitful and illuminating interplay between modern questions and insights and traditional Christian assertions and understandings. There is no intention to seek simply a restatement of Christianity in terms 'acceptable to modern man'. The Editors believe that it is as misguided to suggest that the truth of Christianity depends on what modern man can accept as it is simply to reiterate the ancient formulations of orthodoxy. The vital questions are 'How may we be led to see what is true?'; 'What is the nature of theological truth and how is it related to other kinds?'; 'What resources have we for understanding and meeting the real needs of men?'; 'How does Christianity look in the light of our answers to these questions and how does Christianity contribute to these answers?'

We hope that this series may be a modest contribution towards *aggiornamento* if not reformation.

iv

Contents

Preface

THE CHAPTERS in this book are a somewhat expanded version of lectures delivered at Sion College in London in Lent 1968. I am grateful for the invitation to give these lectures and for the permission of the authorities of the college to publish them in this expanded form. I am also grateful to the large number of laymen and clergymen who listened so patiently on four successive Mondays to what I had to say.

I have sought in this book to analyse what I have called 'the Christian situation' in the present day, attempting to set the Christian faith in the context of contemporary society and to suggest ways in which, without damage to the integrity of the faith, it may speak meaningfully to those who live in a secularized and 'one-world' community.

There have been many other books, of course, which have discussed much the same theme. But I must confess that I find few of these books satisfactory. It seems to me that all too often they either fail in maintaining what I have just styled 'the integrity of faith' or they fail to see that re-conception, in a radical sense, is required if such integrity is in fact to be maintained. In other words they are victims of what Dr John Robinson has called the reactionary or the revolutionary fallacies. In the former instance, they assume that the simple re-assertion of the old position will do the job; in the latter, they would seem to be prepared to jettison the abiding emphases in Christian history and present us not with a re-conceived but with an entirely new notion of what Christian faith professes. Like Dr Robinson, I believe that what is needed is a *radical* approach. For 'radical' means 'at the roots'; and what we require is a penetration to the basic, enduring, 'root' realities of Christian faith. At the same time we must face the world as it is, without succumbing to nostalgia for what has now gone for ever and without utopian ideas of what is supposed to be coming in the future.

I cannot end this preface without thanking a number of friends, especially younger ones, both in Britain and in the United States, with whom I have talked about these matters during the past few years. More especially I am indebted to my research students in Cambridge University, who have enabled me to sense the 'feeling-tone' (as I might put it) of younger people who combine genuine dedication to Jesus Christ and the Christian community of faith, with an unfeigned and eager acceptance of the contemporary world, in all its strangeness and all its challenge. Their humility and their courage give one hope that the 'Christian situation today' is nothing like so gloomy as some of our professional pessimists would appear to think.

NORMAN PITTENGER

King's College
Cambridge

1. What **is** the Situation?

EVERYONE knows the story about Adam and Eve, thrust out from the Garden of Eden. Bewildered by the strange world outside the Garden, Eve turned to Adam and commented on how different things were from life inside. 'Well, my dear,' Adam is made to say, 'we must always remember that we live in an age of transition.'

The point of the story, of course, is that every age, in every part of the world, represents in one way or another the imposition of change and the requirement that men and women adapt themselves to that fact. But if it is true that every age is an age of transition, it is certainly the case that in our own time we are most vividly, even painfully, aware of the fact. To say this is but to repeat a commonplace; none the less, it *is* true that we have today this enormously aggravated sense of transition and that we must recognize that for many of our contemporaries, perhaps for ourselves, it is not easy to accept. Yet facts are facts and it is required of us that we take them for what they are and attempt to come to terms with them.

Not only is the world situation changing rapidly, more rapidly than it has changed in other periods of history. The older stabilities, particularly the 'religious' ones, are being swept away – or so it seems. In some ages, at least the orientation of men towards what they regarded as transcendent – and hence as offering them what Professor Farmer has taught us to call demand and succour in our time of trouble – was unchallenged and unchanging. Thus there was something to which appeal might finally be made; there was something which could unfailingly be relied on, seen as an abiding refuge. Hence, when the going was hard, there was a reality which could give a certain 'firming-up', an awareness of persisting structure, when all else appeared confused and confusing. There was something to which men could turn with confidence, finding reassurance and help in their moments of perplexity. Nowadays, however, most of us do not have even that sort of stability to which we can turn; certainly for vast numbers of people, *everything* seems to be in flux. They feel lost, lonely, insecure. The words of the poet are appropriate to describe their condition:

> Lonely and afraid
> In a world I never made.

I have said that much of this picture is a commonplace. Why then do I speak about it? My excuse is that during the past ten years, thanks to a number of contributing factors, I have been able to travel very widely and hence to observe ways in which this situation manifests itself in many parts of the world. For more than thirty years I lived in New York City, as good a place as any to get a feeling for what is going on; I have spent much time in other parts of the United States, in Puerto Rico, Hawaii, and Canada; some years ago I was in New Zealand and Australia for a considerable period. Since coming to live and work in England, four years ago, I have travelled extensively on the continent and lived for longer or shorter periods in Italy, France, Spain, Holland, West Germany, and the Scandinavian countries. I say all this simply in order to indicate that my interest and concern have not been restricted to one particular country or to one special set of circumstances. What I shall attempt to do, therefore, is to portray the situation today, in this 'time of transition', as I have seen it reflected in many different places, in many different ways, but always with what I believe to be certain similarities or identities. Inevitably, my major concentration is on English-speaking lands; but I shall not forget, even if I do not frequently mention, other lands.

My purpose in these chapters is not to do over again what has been done so many times before—to sketch, so far as may be possible, all aspects of contemporary culture which have a bearing on the pattern of change in our time. Our concern will be related to one big question: how can one believe and live, as a Christian, in such a world as that which is ours today? Phrased slightly differently, our concern is to understand what the changing order of things, in its many aspects, suggests in respect to the abiding assertions of Christian faith and Christian life. Or, to put it in still another way, is it indeed possible to maintain, in our own age, the perennial Christian convictions about God, man, and the world, and to live in terms of those convictions?

It is obvious that I am convinced that it *is* possible; other-wise, I should not be writing this book, based as it is on lectures delivered to an audience of Christian believers or those who still wished to be Christians even if they found it very difficult to commit themselves fully in this age of

3

perplexity and confusion. At the same time I am sure that the situation in which we find ourselves requires a very considerable re-conception of what it means to be a Christian. And to say that implies, for me at any rate, that it requires also a very radical re-conception of what Christian faith is all about, what are the demands in terms of Christian living, and the orientation which we must take in respect to the world and human existence. In later chapters, these matters will come up for extended consideration. At the moment, in this chapter and the next, it is my intention to present certain points that seem to me of the first importance. If we are to relate the gospel, and along with it the life which the gospel expects, to the world in which we live, we must have some idea of what sort of world that is. Hence I wish to speak about what seem to me to be dominant motifs in our contemporary culture and then to say something about the characteristics of what we have learned to call our 'secularized' existence today. These two matters will engage our attention in the first two chapters of this book. Only then will it be possible for us to proceed to a discussion of man and the world, as we may understand them today; an attempt to disentangle the valid meaning of 'religion' as a possibility for us, even in a 'secularized' society; and, in two final chapters, the way in which Christian faith 'fits in' and how it may be re-conceived in modern fashion. And let it be said now, so that it need not be repeated again, that I have no desire to attenuate or 'reduce' the reality of Christian faith – I believe that when one takes from anything that specific quality which makes it a *something* what one will have left is nothing worth bothering about. If I have any criticism to make of *some* essays on the subject, it is that they often appear to me to be just this; the result is an eviscerated faith, with no cutting-edge, with nothing

4

distinctive, with no demand or challenge. What I want to urge is a way of seeing Christianity, thoroughly re-conceived for us today, which will ask for the *whole* of a man's allegiance. It was Thomas Henry Huxley, the Victorian agnostic, who once said that 'it may not take much of a man to be a Christian, but it does take all there is of him'. The only Christianity in which I have the slightest interest is a Christianity that 'takes all there is' of the man who accepts it. Our problem today is to make it possible for him to accept it, living as he does in a world in transition, in a 'secularized' culture, in a different situation from that in which his faithful ancestors in another age lived their lives and accepted, with all *their* hearts and minds, the faith which is called Christian.

I begin, then, with a consideration of four points which seem to me to be of quite special importance in our own time. In one sense, these four points are obvious enough; yet I have never seen them brought together and treated as characteristics of the situation in which today we find ourselves.

These four points are: (1) the increasing reliance on science, its attitudes and its accomplishments; (2) the provision for most of men's needs through welfare services and other agencies, often of a governmental sort; (3) the demand, found especially perhaps among younger people, for freedom of self-expression rather than for obedience to conventional codes or practices; (4) the decline of organized religion, in the accepted sense of those words, in almost all parts of the world, but especially in the western countries.

We begin with a recognition of the increasing reliance on science and the enormous respect felt for its attitudes and its accomplishments. Certainly this is an obvious fact in all quarters. It is the scientist to whom multitudes turn when they think of the *real* expert. The authority of science is very largely unquestioned; its supposed deliverances are accepted without hesitation. I recall an advertisement in a weekly journal, showing a man in the white jacket of a laboratory worker. He is holding up his finger, as if he were making a point in an argument. Underneath the picture appears the caption: 'Ask the man who *knows*.' In an earlier day, it might have been somebody else who represented 'the man who knows'; perhaps it would have been a clergyman or a professor of the humanities. Today, for vast numbers of people, the scientist alone can take this position, as of right. Popular wireless and television programmes illustrate the same point. When there is a discussion in which there are men or women occupying posts in scientific departments of our universities or well-known for their researches in other institutions, it seems always to be their views which are heard with respect; it is taken for granted that they know what they are talking about. One might say that scientists have become the 'high priests of our age'.

Science has changed men's lives. It has given them new knowledge which brings with it new power. It has provided them with the possibility of such control of nature as was never before envisaged. It has not only enabled us to destroy ourselves and our planet in a fashion that is terrifying to the imagination and disturbing to the emotional life of every man who is aware of this appalling possibility; it has also enriched life in many ways, by adding greatly to the comforts and conveniences which, in western lands at least, are now taken for granted. It has altered our way of seeing ourselves and the world – altered it so radically that we might almost say that today men are like new creatures living in a new kind of world.

What is most apparent to us, of course, is the technological aspect of the total scientific enterprise. The society in which we live, particularly in Britain and Europe and in the Americas but in its degree elsewhere as well, has been styled 'the cybernetic society'—it is the society in which, through a great variety of mechanical devices, through the use of computers, and through all sorts of apparatus or equipment made possible as a result of scientific study and development, men and women feel themselves less individuals who count, each for himself, and more as units which form part of an intricate technical system. The system increasingly does their work for them. In principle, it releases them for more leisure and for more opportunity to live lives that are rich and full; but what men discover, as a matter of fact, is that by necessity they become in some sense servants of the very machines which the experts have created. Hence there is a certain ambiguity in this high esteem for science, its attitudes, and its accomplishments.

I do not wish to exaggerate. It is unquestionably true that most of us do enjoy more leisure, just as we enjoy fuller lives, with better food, more comfortable living-conditions, and all that might be called the amenities of a technological culture. Nor is it the case that the more men use machines, the less opportunity they have for being truly human. At one time, perhaps, that appeared to be the case; but we are told nowadays that the situation is otherwise. Experts report that as required working-hours get fewer, actual employment does not diminish. We are also told that large numbers of men and women find increasing opportunity for leisure-time activities, which in fact they enjoy and which give them at least the possibility of enriched living. I am not competent to agree or disagree with these findings; I presume the experts know what they are talking about.

Some years ago I attended a meeting whose subject was 'Man's Life in a Cybernetic World'. Those of us who were present were informed that at the present rate of technological development it would require only fifteen or twenty years to bring about a condition, in all so-called 'civilized countries', in which the essential services necessary to keep the population supplied with the ordinary needs of life could be provided if every able-bodied man worked one hour a day, excluding Saturdays and Sundays. We were astounded, not to say appalled, at this prophecy, which was given us with complete assurance by experts in the technological application of scientific 'know-how'. But the scientists who were present did not share our surprise or horror; they asked one question, directed at us who were engaged in education or philosophical enquiry: 'What then do you propose to provide for the people who will have so much free time to amuse themselves, improve themselves, or merely to "exist"?' And that question was followed by another, directed to those of us who were theologians, 'How does this certain development fit in with your theistic beliefs?'

As more and more of men's lives, in all parts of the world, come under this sort of rubric, with this kind of technological advance, it is inevitable that they should centre much if not all their attention on *this* present existence, here and now. This concentration on the present conditions of life is inevitable for many reasons. For one thing, it seems to them that modern scientific advance has made much that was said about 'another world' seem irrelevant, if not actually ridiculous or absurd. But a more important reason is that the ability of the machine to provide for most of the ordinary necessities of life drives them to feel that 'another world', however rationally acceptable and however relevant it may appear in some theoretical sense, simply does not produce results. As I have heard it put, 'It doesn't cut any ice these days to talk about a "future life" when this one is both exciting and adequate.' As we shall see, I do not

8

think that such an attitude makes much sense, in the long run; however we may dislike the putting-off to 'another world' of things that should be done in this one – and I doubt if that is genuinely Christian – the question of man's eternal destiny is linked with the significance he finds in the here-and-now of the present in which he is immersed. But it is obvious that such an attitude as I have outlined *is* very general today.

And I should wish to emphasize my use of the phrase 'in all parts of the world'. No longer do we live in this or that specific place, as if we were insulated or set apart from other areas. Nowadays we all live together and what goes on in one spot is almost immediately felt in another. It is 'one world' today; and when Wendell Wilkie first used that phrase during his campaign for election to the presidency of the United States, a quarter of a century ago, he spoke with remarkable prescience. It is no longer possible for one nation to live out its national existence as if it were alone on the planet; nor is it possible for any man to feel that he can live in disregard of others, not only in his own country but also throughout the inhabited globe. We are all together in the human enterprise and if modern technological advance has done nothing else, it has made that togetherness a patent fact of common human experience.

Inherited religious ideas seem to many today to make no sense. Such ideas are seen, by these people, to be in many respects a reflection of, and therefore meaningful only in relation to, a quite different sort of world from the scientifically oriented, technologically developed, and unitary world which they know. But there is something else which must be taken into account. In a social existence such as that, most of the needs which people feel can be met through the various agencies which the welfare state – or its

9

equivalent, whatever name may be given it – and its associated organizations have set up.

One of the consequences of the Second World War, even in lands which thought themselves immune from such influences, was the establishment of a governmental policy for meeting human needs. It might even be said that the war which was intended to put an end to totalitarian ideas has succeeded in establishing everywhere a certain sort of revised totalitarianism. Let me explain what I mean.

There have been various manifestations of the omnicompetent state. Some of them have been vicious and destructive of human personality. Nazism in Germany, Fascism in Italy, and similar movements elsewhere, set up social structures which denied all freedom to the citizen. Human sociality was turned into something more like an ant-hill than like a co-operative association of men and women who possessed human rights which must be respected. Russian communism and its parallels are not in that category, for despite the abuses which many of us feel present in countries where communism is dominant, and despite the over-riding by ruling cliques of many of the freedoms which we believe to be proper to man, the main objective of these societies is to make possible a very wide sharing of available goods and the establishment of equality of opportunity for the citizenry without respect to class or race or social position. In western countries, such as Britain and the United States, the omnicompetent state has taken another form. In these places the concern has been to secure the provision of all legitimate needs for those who live within the nation's boundaries, to provide the essential social services for as many people as possible, to see to it that there is no unnecessary poverty and that there shall be no under-privileged persons, and in every way to secure the fullest commonalty in public life. In Britain the process is very far advanced, as it is also in (say) the Scandinavian countries; in the United States it has met much opposition, but legislation is moving insistently in that direction and even when theory attacks what is called 'socialism' the reality is indeed a variety of state socialism, with a wider sharing and control exercised for the public good and with an increasing concern to see that equality of opportunity and abolition of want shall be available to all.

In whatever way this has been achieved, or is on the way to achievement, more and more of the needs of men are being met by such agencies. Social services of all sorts are made available; unemployment insurance, old-age pensions, provision for those in want, health services, and the like are part of the picture. Certainly this is all to the good. But one result is that for many persons, especially perhaps for younger people, the old incentives appropriate to a competitive society no longer make much appeal. What is more, when and as essential needs are met in this way and provision is made even for the use of leisure, a very interesting phenomenon appears. It is the demand for self-expression, not so much against or in spite of but as a compensation for the loss of those chances to act freely which an older society offered in its requirement that everyone struggle to secure and maintain a decent existence. This is the third factor to which I wish to draw attention in the contemporary situation.

The so-called 'revolt of youth', including 'student revolt', is quite clearly a manifestation of this imperative demand for self-expression. It is a demonstration of man's desire for freedom in the context of a society which has made many of the older and perhaps less striking modes of self-expression unavailable. The 'provos' in Holland, the *cappeloni* in Italy, the 'hippies' and 'beats' in the United States, and their equivalent in Britain and elsewhere, are all of them concerned to secure self-expression, personal freedom, and the right of a human being to be himself in an environment where he finds most of his needs cared for through public agencies and where all too often he thinks of himself as being, for good or ill, the victim of a pattern which he knows is for the common good but which he finds stifling and restricting.

However odd and disconcerting some of these ways of self-expression and many of these claims for freedom may seem, it would be a failure of imagination and a lack of insight if we did not recognize that the young people in question are desperately anxious to assert themselves as *men*. They are like 'Savage' in Aldous Huxley's prophetic *Brave New World*, the man who demanded that at whatever cost to himself he should be permitted freedom to be himself, to assert or express himself. The 'sexual revolution of our time', as it has been styled, is an obvious example of this. Patterns of sexual behaviour which are simply conformist are linked in the thinking of many young people with a repressive attempt to deny them their manhood; hence they break out in one way or another, often setting up (albeit unconsciously) new patterns of conformity which they accept because at the very least these patterns are their own. The situation is rather peculiar, since the growth of the welfare state has almost inevitably meant that in western lands the moral ideas of the bourgeoisie have been accepted as normative in the very effort to improve conditions and to provide equal opportunity for all. At the same time, it is precisely these ideas which seem to younger people to be dull and respectable, without meaning, a denial of the very freedom which they wish to possess. Robert Louis Stevenson once said that respectability is 'the deadliest gag and wet-blanket' ever devised to inhibit the free spirit of man. Now that such respectability seems to have the sanction of a

whole society, it is all the more likely to awaken a resent-
ment that is bound to show itself in what appear to be
anti-social modes of behaving.

However we explain it, the fact is plain enough. With
the increasing provision of social services and with the
increasing controls exercised by agencies acting for the
common good, coupled with the provision that is made for
material needs and for much of our leisure-time, as well as
the security that is now so widely available, the demand for
self-expression, for human freedom to be and to become
oneself, is more and more prominent. To a greater or lesser
degree, we are all affected by it, however much we may
deprecate the wilder and less restrained modes in which it
shows itself. The more that provision is made for human
necessities, the more that care is offered to those in trouble,
the more control imposed in doing these things, so much
the more likely it is that men and women, sensing their
'creaturely freedom' (as Berdyaev phrased it) shall wish to
find ways in which that freedom may be let out. And in
those areas left to us which we call 'private', our contemporaries believe that they should do what they please, act in
ways that seem satisfying to themselves, be granted liberty
to behave in a fashion which will enable them to *feel* free.

Nor do I think that this urge for and insistence on
freedom, especially in respect to matters that are thought
to be entirely private to the persons involved, is being
exercised in utter irresponsibility. We are often told that
young people demand self-expression without regard for
the responsibility which attaches to all human action. But
the contrary seems to me to be the case. I think that the
younger generation has a quite enormous sense of responsibility, although it is not the conventional idea of what
constitutes responsibility.

For them it is much more a matter of caring for, being

13

concerned about, and wishing to provide opportunities for a similar freedom for other people. Let us not forget that it is these young people who show most devotion to racial integration, political and social rights for all, world peace. It is they who give ardent support to Oxfam, the Peace Corps, and similar organizations. It is they who throw themselves, as they assert their freedom, into movements which work for international understanding; and it is they who are most active in non-violent demonstrations, in resistance movements, and in other sorts of work for a better because more understanding and loving world. Of course there are the occasional outbursts, when in sheer frustration they act in shocking disregard for what most of us conceive to be public interest; but this does not seem to me typical, however much the newspapers may 'play it up', and I believe that the violence can be exaggerated and the stories about that violence very misleading and hence bound to give the rest of us a false picture of what is really going on.

The fourth point to which I wish to direct attention is the unpopularity of 'organized' religion today, not only among young people but in many other circles. 'Organized' religion, as represented by the institutional churches, seems to many to be altogether *too* respectable, too bourgeois; it also appears to them to be on the side of reaction, willing to bless suppression of genuine freedom, tied up with 'power-structures' whose main interest is to maintain the *status quo*. Young people say this loudly; their elders are quieter but often have the same feeling. Religion in its usual organizational forms appears to be a great monolithic force which militates against all genuine freedom, while at the same time it is so out of touch with the scientific advances of our day that it represents 'the good old days' which are now gone for ever. 'The Church' is thought to be 'a bad thing', with little if any promise of improvement in the future. It is to be disregarded or rejected.

Whatever the reasons, nobody can doubt that at all levels and in most diverse ways the discontent with institutional religion is very widespread. But this does not mean that those who reject or condemn organized religion or the established Christian churches are necessarily opposed to any and all religious faith. Much depends, of course, upon the definition which we give to the term 'religion'. But if by that word we mean some awareness of a dimension in human existence which is more than simply human, more than just a matter of social ordering, more than merely decent human living, there can be no doubt whatsoever that contemporary men and women, from all sorts of background, are desperately seeking some possible expression of that persisting awareness. Nor can there be any doubt that among younger people especially there is this urgent desire. Furthermore, there is often an implicit and inarticulate faith, sometimes an explicit one. In my own university the attendance at the special services held for undergraduates is quite enormous; it includes many who would think of themselves as enemies of the organized churches, yet wish to hear and listen eagerly to any presentation of faith which speaks in terms they can understand. And as one travels from country to country one discovers that no single subject is so eagerly discussed, no single topic so readily canvassed, as the possibility of a faith which can help make sense of human experience. Sometimes this expresses itself in odd ways, such as the recent flirtation between popular musical leaders and eastern religious teachers. But more often it is shown in an almost pathetic desire to have Christian spokesmen speak intelligibly and intelligently about what the Christian tradition itself may still have to say.

A striking illustration of the popular mood was the way

in which undergraduates in Cambridge responded to an address by the television personality Malcolm Muggeridge when he spoke not long ago at the University Church. He was devastatingly frank, highly critical, when it came to institutional and organized religion, but he spoke passionately of his own conviction that there is that transcendent dimension of which I have just spoken and he told the fifteen hundred persons present at the service that he felt what he styled 'enchantment' with much that is found in Christian teaching, especially in its presentation of the person and meaning of Jesus Christ. Because he was an 'outsider', so far as established religious groups are concerned, what he had to say seemed to come with particular appeal to his hearers. He was talking about his honest convictions and the response was enthusiastic. For some time afterward, one heard young men and women, and their elders too, talking about what Mr Muggeridge had said. They felt, as one of them remarked, that here was a man who spoke for *them*. They commented on his telling case for *some* genuine religious faith; they recognized and approved the Christian flavour of that faith. And they said that they wished that others, especially those inside the churches, would talk as he had done.

Similarly, I have noticed that when the Bishop of Woolwich and others who may be styled 'radical Christians' come to speak, the reception is identical. It is an enormous help to hear a Christian churchman, and a bishop at that, speak in the exploratory yet convinced fashion of John Robinson and those who think like him. We may not agree with what these men have to say; but the sort of hearing they get makes it entirely plain that religion, in its most profound sense, is *not* dead; it is the organizational, institutional, established (I do not here mean 'the Establishment', the association of Church and State found in Britain)

16

religious groups that seem no longer to receive much respect or, at best, no longer to be heard with interest.

It is not my purpose to develop this point, nor do I wish to present here a defence (which obviously can readily be made) of the necessity for some institutional embodiment of religious faith. I am convinced that without some such embodiment no faith, however vigorously held by this or that particular individual, has much hope of making a real impact. All I am seeking to do here is to describe what we may call a mood. And when it comes to talk about some variety of religion which is entirely 'secular', in the sense of a complete absence of *any* stress on what I have styled the transcendent dimension, my own observation is that there is very little appeal in it to most of my contemporaries, above all to young people. That sort of thing, they seem to feel, despite its claim to be centred entirely in human and hence in readily available interests, to be terribly *in*human. They feel that it disregards the strange awareness of the 'more' in human existence, they believe that no viable religion can be simply and solely concentrated on human affairs. If it is humanism, without any transcendent, that is desired, then (they say) let us have just that, without claiming a religious flavour for it. Yet humanism, in the dress associated with the modern so-called 'humanist groups', does not make much appeal either. Perhaps all this is testimony to the strength of the genuinely religious dimension, still persisting today, even when the usually accepted ways of talking about it, describing it, and emphasizing its importance are rejected as being out-of-date, incredible, and irrelevant for modern man.

So much for my four points. I should like now to call attention to certain other important factors in the contemporary situation, as I understand it.

We are told by many observers that ours is the 'urban

age'. Most of us have read, or read about, such studies of this condition as *The Secular City* by the American writer Harvey Cox. Even if we have not, the massing of vast numbers of people in great conurbations, as they are called, the terrible anonymity of the city, and the emergence of a specifically urban culture, are obvious facts. At the same time, the demand for freedom of self-expression and the reassertion of identity, to which we have already called attention, points up what many regard as a tragic accompaniment of the 'urban age'. People must be together nowadays; often they like to be together. At the same time they know that they require their moments of realization of personal selfhood. Whitehead once said that 'religion is what the individual does with his own solitariness'. His remark has often been misunderstood; it has been assumed that he meant that genuine religion is the denial or contradiction of the sociality natural to man. But that is not the case. The question is what an individual *does* with his selfhood, his 'solitariness', his sense of genuine personal identity. How does one act upon this, how does one realize its meaning, how does one relate oneself as a person to the world in which we live, a world in which other persons also live beside us, with us, for us or against us? How does 'solitariness' get put to work, healthily and rightly? Whitehead was keenly aware of the communal nature of religion in human history; yet he knew that selfhood in each man is both essential and inalienable.

The demand for freedom of self-expression is a manifestation of the deep sense of this inalienable and essential selfhood, which does not contradict but gives meaning to man in his social solidarity. 'No man is an Island, entire of itself': so John Donne said in a memorable sentence. We cannot, we dare not, deny the reality of our human participation, our mutuality, our being and belonging together.

But at the same time, the awareness of selfhood and freedom in selfhood is indelibly human. Our problem is how to deal with the two facts together. Historically the organized religions have functioned to provide some solution. This Whitehead himself emphasized, although he used a different language in saying it. Today, however, these religions do not seem to meet this need for personality-in-community, community-of-persons, as the need makes itself felt for large numbers of people. Yet we may believe – I myself am convinced – that one of the important contributions of a religious faith, with its awareness of the transcendent dimension, is precisely here.

Finally, I come to what seems to me a remarkable and important fact of our time. I refer to the appearance, in all parts of the world, of sheer *good-will*; and I find this especially in younger men and women wherever I have gone. This good-will, as I call it, demands expression and often finds it in very unusual and unconventional channels. With all the violence that one sees, with all the evil that is so obvious, we do not often enough recognize the presence of this 'sheer good-will'; but unless I am entirely mistaken it is not only a real fact but an increasingly significant one. When W. H. Auden wrote the famous words: 'We must love one another or die', he spoke of a necessity which is now apparent to large numbers of people in every part of the world. One cannot 'love to order'; what to me is so remarkable is that this good-will or love has not been manufactured but has appeared, has emerged, in so many quarters.

One quite realizes that to speak in this fashion is to open oneself to criticism and attack. One may be called unrealistic if one stresses such good-will; one may be accused of wearing rose-tinted spectacles as one looks at the world. But I should reject all such negative views. The young people who so often are condemned for their strange clothing, long hair, easy manners, and loose morals, are frequently the very people who are impelled in a surprising way by this good-will. Whatever we may think of their 'love-ins', as they are called, there is something here of deep desire for giving-and-receiving (both together) in mutuality, tenderness, concern – in love. Not long ago we were hearing much about the 'flower-children' who pelted policemen with flowers, who wore flowers in their hair, who wandered about western cities seemingly without purpose – but as I saw them and talked with them, I was reminded time and again of the Italian *fioretti*, 'the little flowers' of St Francis, and I felt in those odd young people something of the simplicity, the desire to care, the urgency to love, which characterized the followers of *Il Poverello* many centuries ago. Of course there were frauds among them. Yet for the most part, what one saw was a reaction against conventionalized, respectable society with all its patterns of superficial decency but hidden ruthlessness, and the reaction was *for* a love which could make life fresh and beautiful.

Not only among youth but elsewhere, we see a new understanding that the only way in which human life can be lived meaningfully is in persuasion, not in force; in good-will, not in coercion; in love, not in hate. This may be idealistic, as some would think; for myself, I am convinced that it is the most profound realism. The insistence on personal relations as central; the demand that in matters of private life one shall be permitted freedom, and freedom to love; the deep insistence on social justice, racial integration, world peace, as required for a world that is to endure – in these ways, and in many others too, there is a manifestation of a love, which I should wish to put with an upper-case 'L' and call Love, as the secret not only of human existence but also of the dynamic of life itself and of the universal movement of things in our world.

If there is to be a new recognition of the quality or nature of that transcendent dimension of which men and women seem always aware, it is precisely through this insistence on Love that it will be found. In a sentimental play of several generations ago there was a line in which one of the characters said to another, 'This love of ours is bigger than either of us'. That character was not talking nonsense; he was speaking of a reality that people feel at their best and most human moments. Love *is* bigger – that is, it is more truly real, more inclusive, more compelling, than anything else in the world; and there is about such Love a transcendent, inexhaustible, and inescapable quality. If we are being told this abiding truth by bearded, ill-clad, perhaps dirty-looking young people; if we learn it from unkempt poets like Allen Ginzburg, the American avant-garde writer; if the conviction is expressed, even forced upon us, by those who act in unconventional ways – so be it. This should not surprise a Christian. For once upon a time, we are supposed to believe, a bearded, very likely somewhat unkempt (by our standards, anyway) and quite probably not exquisitely bathed Galilean workman went about a small country in the Near East, telling those who heard him exactly the same thing, acting in unconventional ways as he expressed in act what he said in word, shocking many respectable leaders of church and state. So much did his life tally with his words, so ready was he to go to the limit (even to death itself, as it turned out) in order to communicate that message of which he was utterly certain in his own heart, that it later became a message in itself: we call it the gospel. And what does that gospel say, when we get beneath or behind its formal phrasing? Surely it says that in that Galilean workman there was an embodiment in human life of a cosmic Love, the cosmic Lover, of such intensity and directness that *there* for those who will look and see, the mystery of the universe was focused in a man's life. 'The Love that moves the sun and the other stars', in Dante's great words, became a Love which brought meaning to human existence and hence redeemed men from triviality, frustration, superficiality, cheapness, and above all from the lovelessness which is their greatest defect.

It may be the case, in an age when science has accomplished so much and yet left us strangely unsatisfied in our innermost spirits, that this message of Love embodied in a man can still speak to us. Perhaps, when we have acknowledged all the benefits of the welfare state and its provision for our human needs and yet find ourselves unfulfilled, that message of Love in a man of our own kind will come to us with freshness and beauty. When in our urban culture as we live in the 'secular city', we think that organized, institutionalized religion is altogether too conventional and respectable, too much on the side of the *status quo*, that message about Love declared in human life will break through to us once again. The upsurge of the spirit of Love in our time, however strange may be its manner of showing itself to us, conceivably could be a working of the deepest and highest reality in the universe. I can only testify that I believe all this to be nothing but the plain truth.

The expression of that spirit of Love may be through secular agencies, for the most part. But the phenomenon of our time, so widely shared both outside and inside the organization of religion which we call 'the church', is the conviction that the supposed gap between the 'sacred' and the 'secular' is an illusion. Indeed one of the reasons for the wide rejection of what is called 'religion', in a pejorative sense, among men and women today is their belief that institutional religious bodies have promoted precisely such an illusion. It may well be the case that some religions have accentuated that supposed but non-existent gulf between 'sacred' and 'secular'. But by its very nature Christianity is and must be a denial that any such gulf exists. Its central affirmation is that the 'sacred' and the 'secular', the holy and the profane, the divine and the human, have been brought together into utter unity in the historical event which is called after the name of the Galilean workman.

In the next chapter, we shall look at some of the characteristics of modern 'secularized' society, the world in which now we all live, in the hope that we may be able to penetrate a little more deeply into the dynamics of that society and thus come to understand how it stands in judgement on much that 'religious people' have regarded as important. We shall hope to see how with all its defects such 'secularized' society provides ways in which the reality of Love, with which true religion is always concerned and in which true religion finds its meaning, may and must be given expression.

If I am right, 'the fields are white unto harvest'. I do not mean that we shall be able to gather into the barns set up by present-day organized religion all that is now burgeoning in the fields. The old barns, as they stand, simply will not serve the purpose for which they were designed and which at one time they served very well. But why should that worry us, unless we are more interested in preserving untainted and unchanged our ideas and preferences, our institutions and our inherited habits and customs? What is important, surely, is that we come to see how 'new occasions teach new duties'. The demand is laid upon us that we be open to new and surprising disclosures of the cosmic Lover. Love is central to life, because it has been embodied once-for-all in life. It may be – I think it is – possible for the old institutions to come to life once again, provided that we are open to Love as it manifests itself, often in surprising and unlikely places; but in any event, it is the Love that matters, not the institutions. Have we faith enough to believe *that*?

2. What Does 'Secularization' Mean?

It has been said, jokingly, that a favourite pastime among certain 'religious-minded' people today is to discover which of them can say the nastiest things about 'secularism' and the evils that it is supposed to bring in its train. While I cannot subscribe to the opposite view – that *everything* which savours of secularity is necessarily right and good – it seems to me that one of our duties today is to understand precisely what has been happening in human society to create the situation which is generally described by that term. What *is* this secularity? what is meant by 'secularism'? and is there any significant difference between 'secularism' and the process of increasing 'secularization' to which attention is frequently drawn by observers of the modern scene?

In considering these matters, I shall not attempt more than a discussion of a few selected points. The factors which appear most obvious today, in association with the so-called 'secularistic spirit' of our age, are so many and so various that several books would be needed – and as we all know a great many books have been written and published – if one were to deal with them in an exhaustive manner. In a moment the five points which seem to me of special importance will be listed and discussed. But first it is necessary to notice something which has been pointed out, often enough, but which still needs emphasis. This is the possibility of a carefully drawn distinction between the 'secularism' of contemporary culture and the phenomenon of 'secularization' which is also a characteristic of that culture. The two terms are often confused; they are used as if they were simply synonymous. But I do not believe that this is the case. Whatever *words* we may wish to employ for the purpose, it is of first importance that we understand that there are two different attitudes, points of view, ways of describing our culture; and the terms 'secularism' and 'secularization' are convenient to use in discussing them.

'Secularism' may be taken to mean the view that the proper concern of man is with his own human affairs, here and now, *and with nothing more*. It is an instance of the 'nothing but' position. The awareness of the transcendent dimension, to which we referred in the last chapter, is simply ruled out as irrelevant if not absurd; there is nothing beyond or above, nothing more and nothing other than human existence – we need not concern ourselves with any matters save those which are definitely and exactly *this*-worldly. What is important is a concern for the right ordering of human affairs, the right relationship between persons, the right use of the newer technology, the right way to disseminate and employ scientific knowledge – this is all we need bother about and all we can bother about, for the simple reason that there is nothing else to bother about. On the other hand, 'secularization' may be taken to mean a process or movement in which the autonomy of human interests is recognized and insistence is placed on our concern with the affairs of this world, with human relationships, with technological developments, and with the dissemination and use of scientific knowledge; but at the same time the possibility of some genuine transcendent awareness is not ruled out in advance. 'Secularization', in this sense, does not demand that we reject, out of hand, the 'more' which for most men is a not easily definable yet inescapably present factor in their experience. What it does say is that this 'more' is not to be used as an escape from the proper recognition and handling of the problems which we face. The transcendent dimension must be recognized and reckoned with, when we come to make an accounting of human life and its interests, yet it is not to be introduced as a way of evading human responsibility. It is not to be brought in as an excuse for not doing our human duty; it is not to be introduced as a convenient alibi whenever human thinking and doing 'gets hard'. None the less, it is always *there* as an abiding motif in human experience; and the change in our circumstances has not demolished the awareness men have of it – I say this in flat contradiction to the oft-heard comment, by 'radical theologians' and especially the 'death-of-God' writers, that the sense of the transcendent has vanished from our consciousness these days. On the contrary, it has only altered in the ways in which it is to be interpreted and fitted into the wider pattern of experience. To deny the presence of that transcendent dimension or to claim that men nowadays do not possess any sense of it in their lives seems to me to be to shut one's eyes to a patent fact. The presence and the potential power of this awareness are an ingredient of human life as every man knows it. There is that 'more' which in his deepest moments he feels, perhaps above all when he is (as we put it) 'in love' – for to be 'in love' is to be conscious, by intimation and hint and often by vivid sensibility, of something that is so much 'greater', 'higher', 'deeper', than the momentary experiences of life that it can only be described as an inescapable reality in which, as a matter of sheer fact, 'we live and move and have our being'.

When it comes to the practical affairs of every-day life, to the planning and working of things, it is probably true that 'secularism' and 'secularization' (distinguished as they must be, one from the other) lead to much the same sort of action. But the difference is there, subtle yet real; and that difference cannot be forgotten or we shall quite seriously misconstrue the situation today.

It is now time to turn to the five factors in our contemporary society which arise, as I believe, from this process of 'secularization' but which do not necessarily lead to sheer 'secularism'. I should list these factors in this way: (1) there is a relative autonomy in all areas of human thought and activity, an autonomy which must be respected even if its relative nature must also be allowed; (2) there is the provision through human agencies of help for men in most of the areas of their existence and this human possibility is to be accepted and even welcomed; (3) there is also the provision, through educational and cultural agencies, of opportunities for men to become more 'adult', insofar as this means the acquisition of important knowledge and the chance of handling their affairs in a more adequate fashion; (4) there is the recognition that our knowledge, valuable and important as it is, is not absolute but always tentative in nature and hence subject to modification as new data are accumulated; and (5) there is an increasing insistence on the necessity for securing, as widely as possible throughout the world, peaceful co-existence and mutual understanding between peoples of all classes, races, and nations, since this is so obviously one world in which we all belong together and must live together. About each of these we shall have something to say. But in saying it, we remember that in the preceding chapter much was said to provide a setting for these aspects of society in its 'secularizing' process. For example, what was said there about reliance upon science and the respect for scientific method, the urbanization of our culture, and the provision through government for human need, obviously has relevance to our present discussion. So also, and especially for the fifth of the points just mentioned, has the recognition of good-will, persuasion, or love as a *sine qua non* for all decent human relations and for all enduring social patterning. Indeed, from one point of view, the five factors with which we are now concerned are only a development of much that has already been said. So be it . . . for the situation in which we find ourselves today, wherever we may live and whatever may be our religious convictions (or lack of them), *is* a situation in which 'secularization' is going on – and it is going on even if we dislike the whole business and wish that things were otherwise.

It is characteristic of our 'secularized' society to insist upon the autonomy appropriate to all areas of human thought and activity. That is the first of the points to which I wish to draw attention. But I have also used, in the listing given earlier, the adjective 'relative' to qualify this autonomy. It is indeed true that more and more we are coming to see that all departments of human life require us to grant them a certain genuine autonomous quality. One might say that there are rules, methods of procedure, appropriate to each of these areas. It is neither necessary, nor is it licit, to introduce an immediately available non-human or non-secular agent to explain what *we* cannot explain, to accomplish what *we* cannot accomplish. In that sense, at least, we have 'come of age' and we must assume full responsibility for what we do, refusing to look for some convenient escape from human incompetence by calling in something beyond or above our human capacities. Furthermore, in undertaking any enterprise which engages our attention, we are called upon to proceed according to the methodology which that particular enterprise prescribes. If we are talking about quanta of energy in the physical world, for example, we must work on the basis of, and in a fashion appropriate to, the given physical data and their interpretation in physical terms. If we are enquiring into economic determinants, we must use both the material and the methods suitable under the circumstances of that enquiry. In every case we must respect what might be styled 'the rules of the game we are playing'.

Each in his own way, Baron Friedrich von Hügel and Paul Tillich laid stress on this point, von Hügel by talking about 'autonomy' in secular fields, Tillich by insisting on the principle of theonomy as against heteronomy or sheer identity of secular interests with divine purposes.

On the other hand, by our using the adjective 'relative' to modify the noun 'autonomy', something important is also being said. The adjective indicates that it is not possible for us to be satisfied with an autonomy which restricts human interests to the *merely* this-worldly or *simply* 'secular'. There is always that 'more' to which I have so often referred. For one thing, the world with which we are inevitably concerned and of which we are necessarily a part is not a series of discrete and insulated entities or areas; everything in it is tied up with everything else. There is an inter-penetration, an inter-relationship, which cannot be denied. Thus in one sense it is true that to understand any single point, the whole context of affairs must be in our minds – not intruded or 'stuck in', as if it were an alien matter, but recognized as present in the nature of the case. If we are concerned with human disease, we dare not introduce external agencies such as 'demons', intruding from some supposedly supernatural realm; to do so would be destructive of the whole enterprise of medical science. Yet we must give due recognition to the fact that in any illness there are many social aspects, emotional and psychological factors, environmental pressures, and the like, all of which play their part and none of which can be overlooked or minimized, even if for the particular and limited purpose which we may have in view they are not immediately relevant or have but a slight significance.

But there is another reason for speaking of 'relative' autonomy. It has to do with that 'more', the awareness of the transcendent dimension to which I have referred. Whether the awareness be vague and dim or fairly clear and compelling, in our secular concerns there is always 'more than meets the eye'. We dare not disregard the whatever-it-is to which that awareness points. Here again, it is not a matter of illicitly introducing, from outside, some supposedly divine activity which is not observable through the instrumentalities appropriate to our work at a given moment; rather, it is a question of whether or not it is *ever* possible to give a complete description of any phenomenon in a fashion that entails no 'remainders', so that we may say, 'This *and nothing else*'. *This* certainly; but the 'nothing else'... 'there's the rub'. In and under every given occasion of experience, there *is* something 'more'. To put it in language borrowed from Gabriel Marcel, there is a mystery about things which cannot be reduced to a simple *problem* about them. Problems are open to our solution by procedures which are suitable for this or that particular set of conditions; we must try to solve them. But when the problem has been solved, the mystery remains. It is the mystery of 'why there is anything at all'; it is the mystery of existence itself; it is the mystery of the relationship between us men who seek to understand and the world which we seek to understand. This is why there is such profound truth in the saying that *wonder* is the only ultimate stance for man as he faces the world in which he lives and as he considers himself living in that world.

Yet for all practical purposes, modern man in his 'secularizing' of life acts as if the rules by which he works in any particular area are there to be respected; they cannot be man-handled or twisted in the interests of some supposed theological principle which may be introduced *ab extra* as if it were a useful tool or technique. Theological principle there may be; I should say, *must* be. But it is given 'in, through, with, and under' (to use prepositions from eucharistic theology) the phenomenal world, not inserted as an alien intruder into that world.

The second point about secularized society has to do with the imperative to employ any and every effort and agency in fulfilling, so far as possible, the human and this-worldly destiny which is ours. It is up to *us* to get to work, not to put the responsibility off on someone else. We cannot rid ourselves of that responsibility by calling in some other agency to relieve us of the necessity to do our best under the circumstances which are ours. Epidemics are to be halted by human effort, not by reliance upon divine intervention. Floods are to be controlled by our taking thought and then the appropriate action, not by supposing that overflowing rivers will be diverted in response to prayer. The feeding of the hungry will depend upon a whole series of human activities, from proper farming through proper distribution, rather than by presuming that manna will fall from heaven if only we put ourselves in the right relationship with deity. In every area human enterprise is the central fact. If we believe in God, we must not suppose that he will do for us, in the sense of 'instead of us', what we have learned to do for ourselves; as the American theologian DuBose once put it, God works not in place of our working but through it and by means of it. Only so can we still maintain the divine activity as a meaningful idea.

Furthermore, our age in its 'secularizing' movement is convinced that the area in which human planning and forethought, human industry and attention, human concern and labour, are essential is an area which is ever increasing in extent. A wholesome and happy and secure existence for ever greater numbers of people in all parts of the world can only be inaugurated if men do their duty – planning, preparing, attending, working, concerning themselves, and making sure that their fellows do the same. This involves also an increasing sense of social responsibility and, associated with it, the recognition that in most quarters of the world (whether their government be communist, socialist, capitalistic) agencies of a public type are essential. Not only is there unwillingness to put off to another life that justice and equality which properly belong to every citizen in every land; there is also an awareness of the need for large-scale effort, demanding governmental or public planning and control, which will make such justice and equality a possibility. What is more, through such large-scale effort by precisely these agencies, what is a possibility becomes more and more truly an actual fact. The basic necessities of life are provided, as well as promised; it matters little whether we are thinking of Russia or Poland, China or India, Britain or the United States – in greater or less degree, with more or less adequacy, that provision is made. The horror of famine is very real, of course; but the remedy is slowly being found and it is being found through secular agencies and by the large-scale planning I have noted. Progress may

33

seem slow; the under-privileged are still with us; whole nations suffer – hence we cannot indulge in cheap optimism. On the other hand, work is being done, plans are being made, programmes are being carried out; there is no reason for total pessimism.

But there is something else. The third fact to which I drew attention is the way in which more than basic necessities are being provided or promised. Educational and cultural opportunities which at one time were reserved only for the specially privileged (whether by aristocratic position or personal wealth) are now made available for the masses. In most countries it is required that parents send their children to schools, either directly operated by the state or conducted by private owners but with standards approved by government. The literacy rate is higher, although it is legitimate to doubt whether the simple ability to read and write can be said to make one an 'educated' person. Those who wish to enjoy music and art are enabled to do so, in more and more places; leisure-time interests, in games and other kinds of play, are open to larger numbers of people. There are child-care, special services for expectant mothers, social security, and the like, all contributing to the well-being of more and more of the world's inhabitants. It can no longer be said that the poor man or the hitherto under-privileged person is without any educational, cultural, and recreational opportunities any more than it can be said that he is denied the medical care and the provision for old-age and unemployment which make life easier and more comfortable. Not enough is being done, we may say; and that is true. But the fact is that *much more* is being done, and by human effort, largely through state agencies, than was ever done in the past, whilst the sense of genuine community responsibility is felt very keenly. The society which is in process of 'secularization' is intent on providing these

34

things for as many members in as many ways as possible. With all the inadequacies which must be admitted, that is the way the world is going today. It is part of the phenomenon which we call 'secularization' and we have every reason to rejoice in what is happening in these areas. Wars, rumours of wars, oppression, under-privilege still exist; racial integration is not yet accomplished and in some countries exactly the opposite takes place; there is much which appals us, and rightly. Yet it would be wrong to stress these matters to the exclusion of the other, more cheerful, aspects of life in the modern world. One can hardly blame those of our contemporaries who look with hope towards the future and are confident that there is 'a good time coming', no matter how dark the picture may be in certain areas today. At the very least, we dare not deny patent facts – and many of these are encouraging facts, even if many of them are much less so.

The fourth point, to which now I call attention as a significant element in 'secularized' society, is the generally accepted view that the knowledge which men possess is never absolute but always tentative, subject to modification as new data become available to us. Such a position is a reflection, of course, of the tentative quality of scientific enquiry and research. Whatever we may have discovered, whatever conclusions we may have reached, every reputable scientist knows that new material will come to hand and hence he does not claim that at any given moment he has exhaustively stated the truth; up to the present moment, he will say, this is how things stand, but tomorrow or the day after tomorrow things may be different. In an earlier day, at least some scientists wrote and spoke in a highly dogmatic fashion: *this*, only this, is the truth, they seemed to be telling us. Nowadays they are much more likely to be a little hesitant and will say that up

35

to the present, so far as they can see, the facts are like this, but there is no guarantee that they will always look that way and we must be prepared to modify our views. Such an attitude contrasts strongly with the absolute tendency which so often has been associated with religious teaching, where it has frequently been assumed that we have learned, once for all, the truth about God, the world, and man. Dogmatism of that sort is in low repute these days; indeed 'dogmatism' is now a *bad* word, for it suggests the pretension to a degree of certainty that nobody feels can possibly be possessed by any human being or by any human institution however exalted. For most of our contemporaries, it would seem, claims to absolute knowledge look absurd.

If there is one manifestation of the 'secularization' of culture, it is to be found precisely here. Modern 'secularized' man may make exaggerated claims in many ways, but he knows perfectly well that before the vastness of the universe he is very ignorant indeed. What he knows, he knows; but there is so much more to be known that he must be modest in his claims. Furthermore, even what he knows may be, almost certainly will be, altered out of all recognition when it comes to be set in the context of knowledge that the future will disclose. He may be wiser than our ancestors in respect to much that is known about 'how things go'; this is simply the fact and there is no reason to adopt an attitude of false humility about it. But what he does know is 'subject to change without notice', as the old railway timetable used to put it.

I have just said that we are wiser than our ancestors in certain respects. That is true especially with regard to matters in the phenomenal world. Our scientific advance has ensured this. But whether we are wiser than past ages in more intimate and ultimate ways is another question. In our capacity to adjust ourselves to the exigencies of daily life,

36

above all to find a way of existing in what some writers have called the 'border-situations' (bereavement, suffering, death, etc.) and to know how to secure integration of self in some enduring cause or person, we do not seem much wiser – perhaps, even, we are *less* wise. This is a matter to which we must turn when we come to consider the inescapable question, unavoidable even to modern 'secularized' man, of the basic meaning of human existence and the abiding reality to which the transcendent dimension points. On the other hand, we shall not help ourselves or others if we deny the accumulation of knowledge during, say, the last hundred years. Nor shall we do justice to our present situation if we fail to recognize that with all that accumulation of knowledge modern men and women are much less pretentious in their claim to omniscience than were many of their ancestors. Perhaps we may put it in this way: there is a vast increase in what we know, but it is always a relative knowledge. In our world, the possibility of any absolute knowledge is denied; there are no statements which in and of themselves may be taken as unchangeable, unalterable, entirely fixed. In the light of new material that may be at hand or that may become available at some later time, changes will be necessary. And any claim that in the specifically religious sphere we have to do with truth that is 'once for all' must be made, if made at all, in a manner that will take this attitude into account. Unless it *is* taken into account, there is no possibility of significant dialogue between the man who speaks of God and his revelation, on the one hand, and the vast majority of his thoughtful contemporaries, on the other.

Finally, as the fifth factor among those we have selected, I wish to stress the sense of belonging-together, the conviction that tolerance and acceptance are essential to human existence, and the feeling that people of all types, in all parts

37

of the world, must learn to recognize (with no regrets) that there are views, ideas, beliefs, patterns of life, and the like which are different from their own, yet as worthy of respect as their own. Planetary understanding and mutuality, we must see, are necessities today. With this goes a demand for wide tolerance; and this is a reflection of the belief that no single man, no particular people or nation, no one religious faith, no philosophical system, can claim to have comprehensive ('absolute') knowledge of the truth. 'Secularization' in its world-wide sweep has produced this open-ness to diversity; and the open-ness is itself the manifestation of a spirit that may be regarded as in itself a philosophical stance – or better, the acceptance (most often unconsciously) of a metaphysical position. I mean here the belief that only through understanding and sympathy, tolerance and acceptance, can life continue in the world as we now see it.

What I have just said may seem absurd when we consider the violence and refusal to accept other ideas found, for instance, in the Chinese 'Red Guards' and in other similar movements about which we read in the daily press. But I am convinced that in spite of the apparent lack of realism in what I have been saying the fact is that the very violence found in some quarters has its explanation, to a large degree anyway, in what is taken to be a failure elsewhere to permit free development and to recognize diversity. The answer to such violence is not in accepting it at its face-value but in labouring for the wider diffusion of tolerance, understanding, acceptance, sympathy. At least that is how large numbers of our contemporaries would put it.

So much, then, for the five points to which I have wished to call attention. Obviously the approach here, as in the last chapter, has been highly suggestive and in no sense has pretended to be exhaustive. It is apparent that in the areas which we have chosen much more could have been said. It is also clear that there is one ever-present danger in each of those areas: there is the minimizing, if not the outright denial, of the tendency of men to seek their own satisfactions, to establish their own attitudes, in such a fashion that they disregard (or *may* disregard) the interests, rights, and welfare of others and even their own best good. In other words, what is absent from secular society, even from 'secularized' society, is a strong sense of what religious faiths have intended to denote when they spoke of man's 'sinfulness'. In reaction from the pessimism which was often characteristic of an older age, modern man is likely to be overly-optimistic about himself, his society, and the prospects for both. This can be illustrated from each of the areas of which we have spoken in this chapter.

Granted that autonomy must be accorded to every field of human thought and endeavour, it remains true that pretentious claims can be made about them. The scientist can be as falsely self-centred as any other man. In claiming autonomy for his subject, he may slip into making claims for himself, his methods, his concerns, which will amount to saying that he and he only shall be judge of the importance and value, even the truth, of his subject. So likewise in providing for human need, leisure, education, etc., through social agencies, it is possible so to think and act that the satisfaction of human need becomes an end which is thought to exhaust possibility – human life is seen in a shallow way, while those who provide the requisite help may became manipulators of the persons whom they are assisting – a tendency all too obvious in some social-workers and social-planners. Again, the provision of opportunities for education and cultural growth can be perverted into subtle indoctrination or the substitution of facile satisfactions which disregard the deeper needs of men. The awareness that all our knowledge is tentative can lead to a cynical, sceptical, superficial attitude, while *any* standards of behaviour can be regarded as silly or useless. Tolerance, with its grounding in sympathy and understanding of others and of their views, can and often does lead to a purely *laissez-faire* attitude, in which nobody is prepared to take a stand for anything; the result may be a triumph for what is worst rather than best for men, instead of an urgent desire to assist them in realizing that best which is available to them and which they may be able to realize.

Yet I find great encouragement in the awareness of the imperative to love and in the recognition of the truth in Auden's lines, already quoted: 'We must love one another or die.' There is a hint here of a vague but genuine knowledge of an absolute of another kind from that which men pretentiously claim. In granting autonomy, in providing not only for welfare but for education and cultural development, in recognizing human knowledge as largely tentative, in accepting other men with their particular views, there is a sense in which love is seen as better than hate, persuasion as better than coercion, and the way of understanding as better than the way of prejudice and arrogance.

Secular man in his 'secularized' society blunders along; he makes mistakes and he acts often in blindness. Yet there is the strange, not always consciously known, and certainly not always concretely expressed conviction that somehow or other goodness or love *is* better than evil and hate. Sinful tendencies and tragic distortions may not be recognized as they ought to be; but secularized society bases itself even if in ignorance on what a Christian would wish to call the doctrine of creation with its corollary in the goodness of that creation despite distortion and sin. Furthermore, this pervasive sense of the importance, nay the absolute necessity, of love in human relationships and of acceptance of the world may point the way for us to arrive at a deeper and more meaningful definition of what religious people call 'sin' as well as a better grasp of what God intends men to become as his responsible children. To such matters we shall return in our later discussion.

Much of what has been said in these two opening chapters may appear obvious to any who are perceptive about contemporary affairs. Yet it is good, sometimes, to have the obvious re-stated, since it may enable us to come to terms with important matters that all too often we are likely to overlook. It is also true that without some such portrayal of how things are today, we are in no position to speak about Christian faith in terms which will make sense to our contemporaries. That faith does not exist in a vacuum; it exists in the world, is intended for the world, and must be understood in terms of the world. This does not mean that it is to be tailored to suit the world's prejudices and opinions; it does mean, at the very least, that relevance is an important element in our approach to the abiding truth which (as Christians we are sure) the faith affirms. And this brings us to a consideration with which this chapter will conclude.

One of the serious difficulties about Christian preaching, teaching and witness today is that far too many of those who are the most vocal advocates and defenders of the faith do *not* seem fully aware of the world in which, like the rest of us, they are living. It is not that they are 'at ease in Sion'; they are not at ease. Who can be, these days? Rather, the problem is that they seem to have little touch with how the vast majority of their contemporaries think and act. Hence they are not heard, even when they speak eloquently and ably about the deepest concerns of the historical Christian tradition. The problems with which they seem to be working are not the problems of which those contemporaries are keenly aware. The gospel which they so earnestly and zealously proclaim does not have contact with the situation in which those contemporaries find themselves. I find this the most disquieting aspect of our contemporary Christian situation.

When one reads some popular religious journal immediately after reading a weekly periodical discussing public affairs, recent books, and the like, one feels that one has entered a strange sort of 'religious' enclave. In that enclave there is much that is interesting, but somehow or other it all seems very unreal. The questions which are raised, the issues that are discussed in editorial and correspondence columns, the news that is reported – all this has about it a 'never-never' quality; it is not related to the questions and issues and events that are vital in the world of which and to which the secular journals are speaking. There is a 'catacomb' mentality in the so-called 'religious world' which suggests that those who live there do not understand, perhaps are not even aware of, what is going on; there is an absence of what one might style the 'vitalities' of ordinary human experience. Above all, there is a concentration on ecclesiastical 'house-keeping' which gives an air of fairy-land to the discussions. Here is a world in which a few good men and women exchange ideas, sometimes with good-will, often with extraordinary heat. But it is *not* the world which most of us know, nor is it the world in which (surely) those very men must spend most of their working lives.

Many years ago, a friend of mine wrote an essay in which he stressed the need for seeing that 'the given gospel' speaks to 'the given world'. He pointed out that while there is indeed a perennial and unchanging element in the faith which the Christian community is to proclaim – hence there is a 'given gospel' – there is also a situation or condition, a 'given world', in which and to which that gospel is

42

to be announced. He insisted that there is a necessary relationship between the two. The gospel is an answer to questions which are posed by human existence, but the way in which those questions are posed will be determined by the situation in which men find themselves. And the answer which is given to the questions, thus posed, will be determined, in some degree at least, by the way in which the questions have been put. The answers in and of themselves will not be found in the questions posed; to think that would be absurd. Yet it cannot be doubted that (as Reinhold Niebuhr once remarked) there is nothing quite so meaningless as an answer given to a question that has not been asked. Or to phrase it better, the way in which the answer is to be given must be related to the situation to which it speaks and must have some relevance to the question that is proposed.

Relevance is not to be identified with truth. It cannot establish truth. But truth which is irrelevant is truth which to all intents and purposes has no sense; it might just as well not have been there at all. Thus we may say that a first condition for the effective re-establishment of Christian faith in the world today is a vivid awareness of that world as it actually is. Every religion has claimed to have a relationship to men and their world; no religion has thought of itself as existing in a 'cloud-cuckoo' land with no such relationship. It requires but a little careful questioning to discover that for many many people today, what goes on in church circles seems out of contact with what goes on in their lives. They do not criticize 'religion' on theoretical grounds, so much as because it appears to them to deal with issues which are to them quite meaningless. High-minded theologians have no right to dismiss such a feeling as lacking significance because faith cannot depend on how people feel. On the contrary, it is their duty to understand how people feel; then, only then, can they show that faith is not only 'relevant' but essential to true and authentic human living. And if Christian faith is not of *that* order, we ought to admit it frankly and look around for something better, by which men can genuinely live.

It may very well be the case, as some recent studies have demonstrated, that the actual number of those who attend church-services, if only occasionally, has not fallen off so badly as some have thought. It is certainly true that much of the aura of Christian morality and some of the more generalized aspects of Christian belief are still present in many lands which once formed part of 'Christendom'. But to assume, from such facts, that the response in depth to institutional religion remains as it was in Victorian times would be utterly unrealistic. Many people may still go to church now and again; more people may be influenced, in some dim fashion, by Christian ethical principles and even by Christian belief. But the *impact* of all this upon general public attitudes and general personal conviction is a different matter. That impact, we have every reason to think, is really very slight.

All the more reason, then, for facing the situation honestly, with no attempt to cover up in order to 'save face', and with the fullest recognition that if Christian faith and the principles of Christian living are to play the part which they might and could play in our 'secularized' society, there is urgent need for a much more drastic re-conception of them than many churchmen seem to feel or even to desire. Can that re-conception take place? I should not have given the lectures upon which this book is based if I did not believe that it can. Hence I venture to close this chapter with what may seem an indecently personal paragraph.

I am utterly convinced of the truth of Christian faith. Like most of my contemporaries, I have known doubt and questioning, certainly I have been forced to face the problems which that faith presents to us. I have been obliged to engage in a great deal of re-construction, re-thinking, re-statement, in order to maintain what I take to be the abiding elements in that faith. But that the basic reality of the world is the driving energy of a personalized and personalizing love, supremely and definitively manifested for us men in a fellow Man: to this I must return again and again as all that makes life worth living. So it is too with other aspects of the historical Christian tradition. Question as I must, feel doubts as I do, puzzle as I may, there is something there which is *true* – true not only in my own experience but true because it provides an explanation of what is going on in the world, despite the evil, pain, anguish, violence, and wickedness which I cannot deny. One's whole life is centred in that *something* and one feels impelled to help others to see that there is a glory there as well as a truth, in terms of which (in Clement of Alexandria's lovely phrase) 'our sunsets become a sunrise'. I may be mistaken about it all; life is a risk and I cannot claim absolute knowledge which would relieve me from the supreme venture of faith. But I do not think myself mistaken; and in my best moments, few as they are, I am profoundly certain that I am not. Yet I am equally sure that only if, as, and when that abiding Christian *something* is in touch with men as they are, can it provide for them what it has provided for me – an anchor in my life's quest. That is why I am sure that re-conception is required.

3. How Shall We Understand Man and His World?

W E H A V E noted some aspects of the situation in which we find ourselves today; we have also indicated certain of the characteristics of our society as it undergoes the process of 'secularization'. With this background, we now turn to a consideration of man in his world. There is no possibility of coming to grips with the Christian faith in its modern setting unless we have some awareness of what it means to be human. And let us remember that it is absurd to attempt to talk about man without regard for his world; evolutionary science has taught us what common sense always knew: that man and world, history and geography, persons and nature, belong together.

For far too long a time, religiously minded people have talked about human nature in what is really a very subchristian, even unchristian, fashion. They have said that man is a 'spiritual being' and they have tended to be highly critical of those thinkers who stress the materiality of man's nature and the enormous importance of the various economic, social, and physical pressures which continually play upon him. Many have spoken as if man is a 'soul' who happens for a short time to inhabit a fleshly body, from which condition he will be delivered at death when the body will decay and the human 'soul' will persist in some imagined spiritual realm where bodies no longer have part or place. Hence they have come to think that the fleshy side of man is not of enduring significance; what matters is entirely distinct from, indeed actually separable from, the bodily 'integument' which for the moment happens to be man's.

In consequence of this supposedly 'religious' attitude in respect to our manhood, the concrete situations in which human beings find themselves have been regarded as irrelevant to the question of 'who man is'; and as a further result, many who would consider themselves devout Christians have believed that concern with those situations – especially insofar as they have to do with social conditions, housing, wages, economic patterns, and the like – is not legitimate for the Church. They think that the Church ought to interest itself only in the 'souls' of men and in the eternal welfare of that separable spiritual entity (as they regard it); it is 'materialistic', in a pejorative sense, to feel responsibility for mundane and earthly matters, which after all are irrelevant to the question of man's essential nature.

When one looks at the Jewish background of Christianity and the insistence found in the Old Testament on the fleshly reality of human life, such an attitude is astounding. The prophets were most certainly concerned about the things of this world, about how men lived, about poverty and riches, about all those very 'materialistic' matters. And when one brings into the picture the central assertion of specifically Christian faith, one can only say that the 'spiritual' portrayal of man is a shocking denial of the basic reality of the whole Christian enterprise. For the central assertion of Christian faith is that in Jesus Christ 'the Word became *flesh*'. And the chief action of Christian worship is through the use of material entities, bread and wine, which are taken and used by God to convey to his children his presence and life brought to us in the concrete manhood of that same Jesus. Here is, if not 'materialism', certainly a stress on *materiality*, on flesh and blood and the stuff of the earth. Surely no religion has been so emphatic about this as the Jewish-Christian tradition; it is astounding that people who think themselves to be, indeed *are* faithful Christian believers, should have failed to grasp this and to show proper determination to act upon what they have seen.

Yet it is not difficult to see how this perversion of authentic Christian faith has come about. The early Church was faced with the necessity of coming to terms with the Graeco-Roman world. It was obliged to proclaim its faith to that world. Christians were drawn from groups of many kinds and large numbers of them were naturally influenced by the general religious culture of the time. Inevitably, the way in which Christian thought was formulated reflected ideas then prevalent. Something of this sort always takes place – we see it today, for instance, in India and Africa, where the gospel must be presented in a way which people who have been moulded by the indigenous culture can grasp. The pattern of thought which prevailed in religious circles in the days when Christian faith made its impact on the Graeco-Roman world was a middle or late Platonism; such a pattern was simply taken for granted when one concerned oneself with such questions as the nature of God, the meaning of human life, and the requirements necessary if God and men were to be 'reconciled' to one another. In respect to the doctrine of God, as we shall see in a later chapter, ideas that were hardly congruous

with the basic Hebraic and biblical teaching were incorporated into the developing theology. But above all, perhaps,
it was the doctrine of man which was seriously affected by
the general culture of the time. The difficulty was that in
using the philosophical and religious ideas which were
commonly accepted, it was almost impossible to give full
expression to the strongly materialistic base which is part of
Jewish thought and receives its Christian dedication in the
incarnate life of Jesus and the sacramental worship of the
Christian Church.

The reason for this was that in the non-Jewish and non-
Christian thinking of the time, man was seen as essentially a
spiritual being who was obliged to live for the moment in a
world that was material. That world, and with it the
human fleshly body, were adjectival to man's true essence. It
could even be said (and it was said by some) that the body is
the prison-house of the soul: *soma sema* in the well-known
Greek adage. Salvation must consist, therefore, in man's
being delivered from that bondage. The body was to be
controlled so that it did not interfere with the soul; ideally
at least, the perfect man was the one who in some fashion
had escaped from his body and its demands and was delivered from his linkage with the world of materiality. His
soul could then be re-united with the supreme Spirit,
God; no longer would the body come between the two
entirely spiritual entities, the divine Spirit and the human
soul.

It is altogether to the credit of the early Christians that
they refused to go all the way with such views. They
believed in the incarnation of God in the flesh and they
declined to accept any interpretation of Jesus which would
deny to him his genuine participation both in the bodily life
of man and in the materiality of the world. In one way or
another, they maintained against great odds what in 1 John

49

is called 'the coming of the Son of God in the flesh'. They rejected all docetist interpretations of Jesus Christ – 'docetism', as the word indicates, meaning views which spoke of Jesus' manhood and fleshly embodiment as only 'appearances' and not genuinely real. They insisted on Jesus' full manhood as well as on his divinity. Indeed the story of the christological controversies in the early Church is largely the story of this conflict with a pattern of thought which undoubtedly had its appeal for religious people of the period but which the Christian theologians saw to be entirely impossible when its implications were followed out. We can see how to men who almost naturally thought of themselves as essentially 'spiritual' and who tended to regard their own bodies as an impediment to religious life, with the world too as both less real and less good than a strictly 'spiritual' realm, there would have been a temptation to say that Jesus was indeed human, but that like the rest of us his humanity was 'spiritual'; his 'physicality', as we might put it, was at best incidental to his true nature. Yet the Church entirely refused to say this. It was aware of the absurdity of any such reading of Jesus' manhood; somehow it felt, in its secret heart, that to reduce the stark materiality of the incarnate One would be to destroy Christianity altogether. None the less, the emphasis on 'spirituality' persisted and it expressed itself strongly in the way in which man generally was envisaged and in the attitude which was taken towards the flesh and towards the world of nature. Responsible theologians were very careful, of course, but for vast numbers of men and women – and of this there is absolutely no doubt at all – there was a feeling that human flesh was an embarrassment and that the world was not really a very good place. Flesh and the world were subject to corruption; they were mortal; even if sin was to be found centred in the human will and in human decision, the flesh and the world were its *seat* – and in some instances a hellenistic reading of certain Pauline passages could make this notion extremely powerful.

So it is not surprising that Origen, to take but one example, had a very peculiar idea of what constituted the 'fleshhood' of Jesus. As the *Contra Celsum* shows, he could not go all the way with his opponent and regard such flesh as (if not evil, then) less than good; yet he was prepared to go far enough to insist that Jesus' flesh was not the same as ours. In his interpretation of the account of the Transfiguration, for instance, he speaks in this way. Other, less careful, less biblically oriented, Christian preachers, teachers, and thinkers would go much further; it is not to be wondered at that virginity was exalted above the married state and that the long (and tragic) denigration of human sexuality had its start at that time. I think that one might phrase it in this way: the Christian thought of the time never denied or denounced human flesh, the world of stuff, and sexuality in man, but it really did not like those things and rather wished that God had made us and our world otherwise.

Despite the insistence of the Fathers on the embodied manhood of Jesus, the way in which our Lord was understood by great numbers of Christians was as an almost entirely 'spiritual' being. Even when his physical resurrection was maintained, as of course it was, the 'spirituality' of the risen body was stressed. We have our own difficulties with the stories of the physical resurrection; but we can see that they had one merit, if nothing else – they ought to have made it very clear that materiality *counts* in God's purposes. But the excessive stress on spiritual aspects of Christian faith and the view that man is essentially a 'spirit' or 'soul' prepared the way for ideas about human survival of death in which the strong Jewish and biblical emphasis on the utter necessity and the genuine goodness of human fleshliness and the natural world which is ours was lost to sight and a conception of 'eternal life' as meaning simply and solely the 'immortality' of that human 'soul' was substituted for the specifically biblical picture of 'resurrection'. Only in a few cases, notably in Tertullian, was materiality maintained; and with him the materiality was of a very primitive sort indeed.

In post-patristic thought, through most of Christian history, this 'spiritual' picture of man has persisted; and to such a degree that for most people it is actually identified with Christian teaching. Certainly this need not be argued; it is patent to us all. Even in our own day, the same idea continues to be held, so that in most Christian circles it is simply assumed that man is a compound of two entities, a 'soul' and a body, which at present are together but which are separable. The body, where the 'soul' dwells, is *less* important than that 'soul'; and for many this means also that the world of sticks and stones and stuff is *much* less important than supposedly 'spiritual reality'.

In our 'secularized' society, any such notion is bound to be rejected. The harsh facts of life have made it incredible. Religious people, of a certain kind, may still think that their concern is with the 'soul'. Other agencies may look after the body and its needs; other agencies may also pay attention to the world of matter. The division seems quite neat, but obviously it will not work, since as one of our own poets, Robert Browning, once put it:

... 'All good things
Are ours, nor soul helps flesh more, now, than flesh helps soul.'

In any event, in a 'secularized' society, we know that bodies *do* count. We know that what happens to and in the body, what takes place in our material or natural environment, is of prime importance in determining what happens to and in, and what takes place for, whatever-it-is about us and the world that is non-fleshly, non-material, of the order of 'spirit'. Nor is it only what we have styled the harsh facts of life which teach us; it is also all that we have been learning about psychosomatics, the close inter-relationship or inter-penetration of mind and matter, spirit and stuff, intelligence and thing. Both in respect to human health and to human illness, we function as whole entities, organisms in which thinking and bodily sensation are most intimately associated. As the French philosopher Gabriel Marcel once put it, we do not *have* bodies; we *are* bodies – just as we do not *have* minds but *are* minds.

Nowhere is the misunderstanding about human nature and its setting, about man and his world, more seriously evident than in the matter of human sexuality. 'Love is a matter of man's spirit', it has been said. But the truth is that love is a matter of man's total personality in its organic wholeness. Human love is not only spiritual; it is inclusive of man's total physical nature, his chemistry and biology, his psychology and his physiology. When this is not understood, we see the preposterous assertion, made supposedly on behalf of Christian truth, that at its best human loving is a disembodied experience. And then, when the obvious natural (and hence physical) expression of human love, with the desire for physical contacts of one sort or another, comes into the picture, those who hold the 'spiritual' interpretation to be the only properly Christian one throw up their hands in horror and denounce the terrible sinfulness of what they see. In but one area can there be physical expression, they say – an admission that in some circles appears to be almost unwillingly given. That area is within marriage and even within marriage only when the procreation of children is in view.

Certain recent controversies within the Roman Catholic

53

Church have brought all this to public notice. But despite the wiser and healthier attitude taken, say, by the Anglican bishops in their report on marriage and the family, published more than ten years ago, along with similar statements from other Christian groups outside the Roman Catholic Church, the idea still persists that all Christians *ought* to be 'against sex', as it has been phrased. On the very day in which this chapter is being prepared, a writer in the London *Observer*, himself evidently not a Christian, says flatly that 'Christians are ambivalent about sex,' tending 'to disapprove not merely of the hurly-burly on a chaise-longue but even of the deep peace of the marriage bed.' He goes on to put it even more strongly. Despite the 'official teaching,' he thinks Christianity throughout its history has entertained 'hostility' and 'suspicion' in regard to human sexuality, its 'resounding saints' (he mentions Gregory, Augustine, and Ambrose) have 'viewed the whole business with fastidious distaste and accepted it as a regrettable necessity,' and (with certain 'accommodations' in Protestant, Greek Orthodox, Ethiopian, and certain Roman Catholic circles, which he allows) the main stress has been that human sexual activity is 'not for pleasure and not even for the maintenance of a happy relationship between a couple,' but 'has only one purpose, utilitarian, essential, and admittedly unreliable, i.e., the procreation of children' (all quotations from Patrick O'Donovan, writing on 'Sex, Sin, and Catholics', *The Observer* 4 August 1968).

My reason for this long excursus is simply to show that whatever may have been said 'officially' within the Church, the impression is very widespread that the Christian attitude towards human sexuality is essentially negative. There can be little doubt that even today many Christians still talk as if chastity, which they interpret as abstention from all overt physical sexual acts, is the ideal state for man. As a conces-

54

sion to human weakness and in order to secure the continuance of the race, such acts may be permitted for married people. The inevitable result has been the suppression of physical sexuality by many who think that in so doing they are acting in a specifically Christian manner. Such suppression has produced, within some Christian groups, a warping and twisting of personality. This is not always the case, of course, for there are people who can find ways in which the natural physical expression of the drive of human love may be re-directed without damage to personal integrity – monks, nuns, those who for vocational reasons choose to refrain from all overt acts, and some who bring themselves to do the same because for one reason or another they cannot marry, are cases in point. Yet it would not be wrong to say that for the great majority attempts at suppression bring about a distortion of personality, instances of which are seen in the so-called 'spinster' type – the man or woman who narrows his or her life and becomes embittered in the depths of personality. Thank God there are those who by some special grace are delivered from that fate; but there are many who are not delivered or who cannot deliver themselves from it.

In this situation we should not be surprised by the increasingly large number of men and women, perhaps particularly younger persons, who demand the right and take the opportunity to express their sexuality in ways that seem shocking to the respectable. We live in an age when the general pattern of Christian belief has come under severe criticism, when the conventional moral patterns appear unreal, and when the vitalities of human existence have re-asserted themselves with extraordinary vigour – this last for reasons we have already noted. Human nature, with its inevitable sexual aspect, cannot be repressed for too long. Indeed, even during the ages when at least lip-service was given to what were supposed to be Christian sexual principles, the facts often did not run parallel with the professed ideal. One has only to read the medieval penitentiaries to see that sexual behaviour in 'the age of faith' did not come up to the standard which had been set for it; otherwise, the detailed discussions in those documents would not have been required. Now that there is much more open-ness about the whole matter, along with readiness to question the validity of the standard itself, it should not be an occasion for wonder when we find men and women, boys and girls, 'breaking out' as they do.

It is not my intention to advocate a simple acceptance of 'what everybody does'. The problem of a sound and viable Christian sexual ethic remains with us and one of the tasks of modern moral theologians is to work one out. But we dare not talk about the subject as if we were concerned with spiritual beings whose bodies are at best to be controlled and at worst to be subjected to severe repression and even punishment. If we hope to make any sense of human sexual behaviour, we must face the reality of man as an embodied being, all compact of thought and emotion, of physical urges and psychological drives; and my reason for speaking about human sexuality is simply to urge that in this particular area, perhaps more plainly than anywhere else, we see how the strictly 'spiritual' view of man is neither truly humane, soundly based, nor properly Christian. In a word, that view is sheer nonsense. I have quoted Gabriel Marcel's saying about man's *being* rather than *having* a body. This seems to me plain fact, just as it is also fact that man is an intelligence and a will. Above all man is a *desire*, a strong and indefatigable yearning for fulfilment and self-fulfilment. But about that we shall say more at a later point in this chapter.

Man is a body. He is an intelligence and a will; he is a desire. He is also a focus of relationships – a social being. It may be that the two false ideas go together; the notion of man as 'a soul' may lead to the notion that he is '*an* individual' who could exist entirely apart from relationships. But whether or not the two are logically related, the idea is still prevalent in many circles that man is to be characterized as so much an individual that his social belonging, his 'withness' in the sociality of the race, is relatively unimportant. Yet here once again the biblical understanding of human nature and our commonsense experience are in complete agreement; both declare that no man can be explained save in his relationships with others, both see that his very existence is a social existence. We are constituted by our relationships as much as by whatever specific identity we may possess.

I have suggested that the notion of a 'soul' and the notion of an exclusive individuality may be related. Certainly it is true that many religiously minded people, intent upon the 'soul', have thought that *my* destiny, *my* salvation, is what matters most; they are convinced that the purpose of Christian ministry, for example, is to aid in the development of that individual 'soul' so that its final end may be secured – in heaven perhaps. And a good deal of the criticism made of social concern on the part of the churches has been based on the claim that after all their work should be with individuals and not with social groups. As if the two could ever be seen in separation!

Doubtless none of us is enamoured of the kind of totalitarianism which has little respect or care for this or that given man or woman or child. Yet it is worth observing that the extreme totalitarian emphasis in recent years and in some quarters of the world may very well be the result of a violent reaction from the kind of individualism which has

57

so often marked western society. When a former president of the United States, Mr Herbert Hoover, insisted that we should regard what he described as 'rugged individualism' as the peculiar heritage of Anglo-Saxon culture, he was in fact talking about one of the worst things in our history, even if he himself felt that this view of human nature (and the results of it in social life) was altogether to be commended and defended. Whatever else a man may be, he is *not* a 'rugged individual', save when he is in profound defection from his concrete nature as man. For we belong together, we are dependent one upon another, and we cannot live (even if for a time we may manage to 'exist') in separation or isolation from others of our race. In the fine phrase from the Old Testament, we are 'knit together in one bundle of life'.

Of course this does not imply that we are ants in some great ant-hill, with nothing that is peculiarly our own. It only means that to be a person *is* to be in relationship; it only means that to try to go alone, without dependence on others, is to damage seriously if not totally to distort our manhood. Our picture of human nature must be such that the most serious attention is given to the society of which we are a part. That society is first of all our immediate family and our intimate friends; but it spreads out to include the neighbourhood in which we live, the town or village, the nation, and eventually the whole human race. It looks to the past as well, recognizing our participation in the whole history of the human family; it is open to the future, seeing that those who will come after us are also members together with us of that family of men. We are all of us knit together in the very fact of our being men.

The biblical assertion that the whole race was 'in the loins of Adam' is a picturesque and mythological way of speaking of this collectivity to which willy-nilly we belong.

And for Christians, the insistence on what Professor Moule in his recent *The Phenomenon of the New Testament* calls 'the corporate Christ' is surely a central element in our understanding of what was wrought for us in the life and work of the Man Jesus. We are created persons-in-society; we are redeemed as persons-in-society.

But there is even more. So far we have been speaking primarily of man and human society in what might be called historical terms; yet we need to remember that all history has a geography – that is, history is related to, located in, necessarily involves a given place in the world of nature. What is more, we men ourselves are so made that the stuff of the natural world is ours. It has often been pointed out that from one point of view a man is only a few shillings' worth, perhaps in American currency a dollar's worth, of quite common chemicals which in other forms are scattered throughout the natural order and make up that order – we are made of the stuff of which nature is composed. There are differences, of course; they must not be forgotten or minimized, but it is good for us to be deeply conscious of our belonging to nature – good not only for our human pride, which it will humble, but also for our human understanding, which it will illuminate.

Unhappily, some theologies which have been popular in recent years seem not prepared to stress this. They emphasize history and minimize the natural order. They seem to make man an almost alien visitant on this planet of dust, of chemicals, of natural drives, of general regularities and surprising novelties. But any such theology will not serve us, for it is unfaithful to the biblical insistence that we are 'of the dust of the earth', while those who hold to such a theology fly in the face of what modern science, and especially evolutionary science, plainly demonstrates to be the case.

Now when views like that are advanced – and they are

by no means novel in the history of western thought, not to mention Indian philosophy – it is inevitable that sooner or later there will be a reaction. Today we see just such a reaction; in violent revulsion from historical man, interpreted without his natural setting, we witness a remarkable return to the physical, material, and 'natural'. The reaction can go to extremes; it can produce a negative attitude towards intelligence, thought and rationality, with a vigorous stress on the body and its intimate relationship to nature. It can also lead to such emphasis on material reality that the valuational and appreciative side of human existence and human sociality is forgotten. Yet we should be grateful to the cultists who have spoken of the importance of the body, to the scientists who have portrayed man as most definitely part of nature, and (perhaps above all) to the Marxists who have recovered what so many Christians seem to have lost – the awareness that man is part of an ongoing process of social events and that these events have their inescapable material base. What happens to our bodies, in this extended sense of the word – that is, all that goes to make us up, our physical existence, social belonging, and the world of nature – happens to *us*. We shall never be able to make any sense of our manhood if we persist in locating the *us* in some ethereal spiritual realm, if we dissociate mind or spirit from stuff and sense, and if we fail to see what is so obviously true – that we are one with nature even while we also transcend it in specific ways.

As a man, then, I am a particular 'routing' or process of occasions in the world of nature. I have, or better I am, a memory, establishing continuity and identity with those occasions in what we call our 'past'. I am in relationships which are inescapable for me and which establish in me a sort of give-and-take, a receiving and responding, a giving and a being given, which makes me what I am at any particular moment. And I have an aim or a purpose or a project, luring me towards fulfilment and in that way towards a genuine and enriching *self*-fulfilment (in company with my fellowmen) which is made possible for me if I will permit my strong desires to move in the direction in which they are intended to move. All this is what it *means* to be a man. Here I wish to stress *desire*. The Buddha wanted to be delivered from it. He found in desire the cause of human suffering. He was right in that, of course. But desire is also the occasion for all human joy. The drive in human personality, deeply emotional but much more than *mere* emotion, which brings us to *want* and to want terribly, finds its supreme expression in love; and love, as we shall be seeing, *is* desire at its highest, seeking to give and also willing to receive, in deepest mutuality and sharing.

It is at this point, too, that the contemporary demand for freedom in self-expression finds its explanation. I am the kind of creature that *must* express itself in giving and receiving; I have the capacity to choose whether or not I move in the direction which will bring to fruition that enormous desire.

My *memory* which is the total past which I incarnate and sum up, including conscious recollection but also deep bodily remembrance in my very tissues and cells and drives; and my *relationships* in all their richness, including both my intimates and my more remote associations, including also the nature which environs me, presses in upon me, and provides me a stance as well as giving me the material stuff of which I am made – these two offer me a way of being myself. I can choose that way or I can reject it. I can go in the wrong ways in the wrong direction – which means that I elect to take immediately available rather than longer-range ways of self-fulfilment. If I do this, I shall not come to genuine fulfilment of genuine possibilities for my richest satisfaction. But I may elect the right ways – which is to say, the truly fulfilling ways. As a Christian, I should know that those ways are God's will for me; the others are not. God's will is not imposed *ab extra;* it is simply what Paul Lehmann has so correctly perceived it to be: the purpose to make me and to keep me truly and authentically human. And the duty of the moralist, we may say, is to indicate the right and the wrong directions. The one thing he must not do is to suggest that freedom of self-expression and the urgent desire thus to fulfil self are illicit for man. If he suggests that, he cuts the ground from under his own feet, since if there is no freedom, no right to enjoy it, no responsibility to choose it, no chance to express (and so fulfil) oneself in that freedom, and no licit desire to *become* what one has it in one to become, then there is no morality at all. There may be simple obedience to divine fiat; there may be the re-shuffling of already existent entities which then fall into slightly different configurations; there may be a rigidly deterministic universe – but there is no morality. Morality requires freedom and the desire to be free; and with it, morality implies the novelty of self-hood which every man believes he may attain and which his experience indicates that now and again, at least, he does attain. Yet *never* in utter isolation, always as a man with men, living as an organic whole in the world of nature as well as in the realm of human history.

The word 'organic' has been used several times in this chapter. The reason is clear: if we have such a view of human nature as I have been proposing, we must think of ourselves and of others, and of the human situation as a whole, in organic terms. We must think of the world in those terms, too. But for men, it is plainly true that while we insist on the right of self-expression and on the utter importance of self-fulfilment, we must at the same time see that the self-expression is organic with the fulfilment of other men and that the self-fulfilment is related to the total community in which men live and where they also express themselves. Such a consideration constitutes a criticism of those kinds of self-expression and self-fulfilment which would disregard the good of the neighbour. We may look with concern, therefore, when we see the tendency of some younger people today to feel that they can do *what* they want, *as* they want it, and *when* they want it, with no attention to others. One can understand how they come to this point, in reaction from their experience of the sort of community which represses and negates their self-hood, even when it provides for most of their real needs and offers opportunities for educational and cultural development. But as a matter of fact, those who take this position are on the way to destroying themselves if they assert their self-hood without regard for others in the great community of men. Hence what is so greatly needed in our day is a purpose or goal or ideal or cause which will be compelling in itself and attractive to young men and women, but which will also be keyed to the deepest and best interests of the total community of men in which, however much they or others may forget it, they and all of us are participant.

The entirely proper desire and demand for self-fulfilment can only be healthily expressed, and such self-fulfilment only truly attained, when it is sought in the closest association with the self-fulfilment of others. Therefore that *kind* of drive and desire, in which no such concern for others is felt and in which the larger human community is forgotten, is bound to fail. It seems that the grain of the universe, the way things *really* go, forbids its achievement. It produces but one result: a sense of desolation and loneliness, whose coming may indeed be delayed but which is as certain as anything can be; all that can happen is that there is dust and ashes in the mouth, a terrible loss of integrity, and a more and more miserable sense of having become lost and hopeless. That this is in fact the case is demonstrated often enough by the spectacle of the apparently 'successful' men and women whose inner lives are empty, whose capacity for meaningful contacts with others is reduced to a minimum, and who are anything but the happy people they sometimes pretend to be. They are forlorn, isolated from their fellows; their situation is tragic. For by seeking what they want, they have missed the way to achieving their deepest human desire – the only really human desire. That desire is to be a man. But one can become a man only in rich commonalty, not in elected isolation. We are *made* that way; the attempt to act as if this were *not* the way we are made brings unspeakable loss and a devastating sense of frustration even when outwardly a person may seem to have achieved all that his heart desired.

On the other hand the denial of opportunity for freedom in self-expression and in the choice of ways for self-fulfilment is equally damaging and destructive. It is precisely because many people today have the feeling, deep down inside them, that they are not permitted to be and to act in this fashion, that they break out violently in other ways. Such people may be mistaken in this feeling; often they are. But the call to discipline and order, so frequently made by those in positions of authority, seems to them a denial of their freedom to be themselves. Once again, the need is for some cause, ideal, goal, or purpose which plainly appeals to the healthy instinct for being and acting as a responsible self in community with others, but which at the same time has an 'inclusive' character which can make it available for the largest number of men and women who can be won to support it and brought to give themselves, in all freedom of choice, for its furtherance.

Now it is in this context, I believe, that the love of which

Christians speak has its peculiar quality. Christian love, which by definition is a participation in the love of God brought to men in the Man Christ Jesus, is not the complete opposite of all those natural vitalities and desires which men feel within them. It has sometimes, perhaps too often, been represented as such a denial; yet it stands before us as both the completion and the correction of human striving. Christian love obviously requires the correction of the self-centred attitude that may seem 'natural' to men when they do not know themselves as they really are; but chiefly it is the completion and coronation of man's natural drive to love, to express himself in love, and to find in that expression his own fulfilment while he also contributes to the fulfilment of others. It did not require the work of psycho-analysts to tell us that men wish to give themselves and to receive gladly from others, although we have every reason to be grateful that so many of the experts have made this so plain to us. I shall urge, later on, that man is made to be a lover; his capacity for love is the most profound truth about him. And that desire to love, in all its distortions, is not accidental; it is the heart of the matter. Furthermore, love is always personal and personalizing – what is important is not *what* one loves but *whom* one loves.

When Jesus appealed to the child as a type of those who may enter the Kingdom of Heaven, he may very well have intended to indicate that remarkable capacity, found in children, to be open and trustful, glad to give and equally glad to receive. In any event, the fitting-together, as we might call it, of natural love (with the correction of distortions which are necessary) and Christian love makes quite impossible any view such as that propounded by Anders Nygren when he argues that between 'divine love' or *agape* and 'human love' or *eros* (at best, perhaps *philia* or 'friendly brotherly love') there must be perpetual conflict if not the starkest opposition. That position, it seems to me, is biblically unsound, as the frequent use of the experience of human love (found both in the Old Testament and in Jesus' own teaching) to point to God's love demonstrates. The position is contrary to the best strain in the Christian tradition, which (with all its anti-sexual prejudice and its suspicion of man because of his sin) has yet been 'naturalistic' in rejecting a complete disjunction between God and man – and this despite certain modern theologians who seem to glory in making God so remote and so self-sufficient that he is irrelevant in his world. The position is psychologically impossible, for it is simply not the case that there is no relationship, deep within man, between the passionately yearning and desiring love which is the basic human *eros* seeking to give but also wishing a return of love, and the love which is of God and which is God. On the contrary, according to the principle that we know and share 'divine' reality only *ad modum recipientis* (according to our human capacity thus to know and share), we must recognize that human love is both the reflection and participation of the divine love.

The use of the marriage symbol, the almost excessively erotic imagery employed by some of the saints, the assertion that to love the brethren is nothing other than the love of God: here are indications that divine and human loving are most intimately related. Any pastor knows very well that those who have had *no* experience of what it means to love and be loved, humanly speaking, find it almost impossible to make sense of the divine Charity. And the acute psychological observation behind the Johannine insistence, in the fouth chapter of 1 John, that love of God and love of the brethren must go together, should show us that Nygren's dichotomy is not only unworkable but unchristian.

In a later chapter I shall have much to say about God as

himself Love; here I wish to insist that man too is 'love', or if you prefer it, man is created to became a lover. In his urge to love he is frustrated by the inevitable limitations imposed in the created order; he cannot love universally and there are obstacles (not in themselves evil or sinful) to his full expression of love. Man is also distorted or twisted in his loving, since both ignorance and wilful election of easily available ends prevent his truest self-expression and his proper and divinely intended self-fulfilment. None the less he is naturally a lover. So also in human society, of which we are all a part. Human society is intended to be a society of love – of mutuality, giving and receiving, in all understanding and sympathy. That society can centre its love, as can each man, on a love that is less than universal; but in its deepest intentionality, human society exists only as men reflect and participate in the love of God. St Augustine spoke of the 'two cities': the love of self to the contempt of God and the love of God to the contempt of self. He had hold of a deep truth but he put it in terms which are misleading. *No* love can be totally in 'contempt of God', for all love is somehow related to the creator who *is* Love; and love of God on man's part is not to be 'contempt of self' but for the correction and completion of self. Indeed St Augustine, from his own experience, knew this; when he was not engaged in polemic and when he was not exaggerating in order to make a point, he said it too. Surely one of the finest things he ever wrote was that when it comes to understanding what love in God and love towards God means, 'he who loves will know what I mean' . . . and in that little sentence, his whole life is summed up. For even the love which he regretted, the strange and twisted love of his pre-conversion days when he 'came to Carthage burning, burning' (in Eliot's words), the love of his mistress (how sad it is to read of his treatment of her), the love of his little boy Adeodatus (and how significant that name is), the love of his friend Alypius (his 'other half', whom he could 'never lose because he loved him in God whom he could never lose') – all this contributed to his grasp of the divine Charity which was the centre of his existence, even if he forgot it sometimes when he was in controversy with those whom he considered heretics.

I am pleading for a recognition that man is an organic being, a person-in-the-making, who in his relationships finds fulfilment, who is set in the natural order, who *loves*. I am urging that in this loving his whole self, including body and mind, will and desire, chemistry and biology, self and society, history and nature, come to a focus. The basic question for man is what he makes the heart and centre of his loving; and this involves also how he loves that which he finds 'love-worthy'. What man is to become, in self-fulfilment with others as he expresses himself in love, will be determined by what he loves and how he loves. Precisely here the Christian faith ought to speak to him. It ought to speak in such terms that as a created lover, a frustrated lover, a twisted lover, he can understand what is being said to him. Alas, so much of the time we Christians seem not to speak to him at all, since what we say is cast in a mould which either contradicts what I have been urging is the truth about man or is stated in a fashion that conveys nothing to him.

In the last resort, I suppose, what I am pleading for is a deepened and enriched 'naturalism' in our understanding of human nature, its materials, its demands, its relationships, its defects, its goals, its final destiny. As a matter of fact, 'idealism' is not Christian at all, if by that term we denote a spiritual philosophy or attitude which in all its talk about 'values' fails to see that only *embodied* values are available to us. It is my conviction that authentic Christianity, based as it is on the biblical portrayal of God and man, nature and history, above all based on Jesus Christ as incarnating God and bringing his human brethren into fellowship with God, has few worse enemies than that sort of 'idealism'. For Christian morality the same is true. An ethic which talks about ideals, aspirations, goals, as if they were like distant stars in the sky, is not the Christian ethic. The Christian ethic is 'down to earth', where God has put us and where he himself has deigned to dwell. We need not be more 'spiritual' than God himself; indeed, we *cannot* be.

A 'naturalistic' ethic, in the sense in which I have described it, is the consequence of a 'naturalistic' faith, in the same sense. Unless I am entirely mistaken in what I have been urging, Christian faith and morality are just that. What is more, such a faith and morality can speak directly and with abundant meaning to contemporary people, who will see nothing but moonshine and senseless rhetoric in the presentation of these things so 'heavenly' that poor human beings are left estranged and helpless. God has mixed himself up in this world; as St Augustine himself once said, we do not need to try to climb into heaven to find 'the way' – 'the way' *has come to us* where we are and as we are; it is for us now to 'walk in it'.

All that I have been saying has an immediate relevance, I believe, to the situation today in our 'secularized' society. It is also the only way in which *religion* can make sense. That word nowadays seems to have acquired a pejorative meaning for many, not least within the Christian Church. I wish to urge in the next chapter that religion is not necessarily a *bad* thing; but at the same time I must admit that as often presented it can be and is far from being a *good* thing. We need discrimination here, lest in our dismissal of the bad connotations we lose the good aspects. It is not necessary to 'empty the baby out with the bath-water'.

4. What is Religion?

RELIGION is having a 'bad press', as journalists would phrase it, at the present day. On many sides, from a surprisingly large number of people both within and outside the institutional churches, the very word is likely to be used in a purely pejorative sense. It is thought to signify ideas and practices which are either incredible or harmful. To many it suggests an escape from the world, from reality, from the hard facts of our human existence. Those outside the churches regard it as irrelevant and meaningless; and we are familiar enough with the view advanced by theologians who have taken their cue from Karl Barth – that Christians, when they are faithful to what Christianity *really* is about, must have nothing to do with 'religion', since that is a purely human phenomenon, mostly evil, whose death in the world was accomplished in Jesus Christ. Furthermore, for many churchmen who do not go all the way with Barth, 'religion' is so identified with the social *status quo*, so embedded in a dying culture, that it is to be rejected in favour of some new stance which they are to call by the word 'faith'.

It seems to me that a good deal of this talk is sheer nonsense. One can understand what is intended, at least by those critics of religion and those theologians who speak with some historical knowledge and some genuine perception. They are urging us to distinguish among the various 'religious' possibilities; they want us to see that Lucretius was speaking the truth when he remarked that 'religion' has done harm in the world – or at least *some* religions have done such harm. But the wholesale denunciation of religion appears to me to manifest a strange blindness to the facts and an indiscriminate condemnation of something in human life that (to me anyway) seems inescapable and necessary. In other words, the difficulty is that in the total condemnation of 'religion' there is a failure to recognize what ought to be an obvious fact: that there are different *kinds* of religion, some of them good and some of them bad and most of them a mixture of good and bad. What is required, and what one often does not find, is a sense of proportion. We need to see both the good and the bad in this human phenomenon; and then, having seen this, to engage in the necessary purification which will confirm what is good and reject what is bad. In this connection I should commend the present Archbishop of Canterbury for his careful discrimination between the good and the bad, along with his welcome insistence that the basic truth in the religious stance is an indelible feature of human existence, once man has come to see that he is not a completely self-sufficient and utterly independent being.

The German martyr-theologian Dietrich Bonhoeffer is the writer who is most commonly associated with the outright condemnation of religion so prevalent in our own time. Some phrases from his remarkable and fragmentary correspondence, written in prison while he was awaiting the fate which his Nazi captors had in store for him, have been quoted freely and without regard for their context. Indeed they have been quoted *so much* out of context (and often from the first translation, whose accuracy is questionable) that what Bonhoeffer was intending in his comments has been seriously misinterpreted. When I say 'context' here I do not mean only the fact that Bonhoeffer was in prison and hence under very considerable strain; I mean the entire background and the environment in which he found himself, as a German Lutheran who not only belonged to but had accepted the piety which is distinctive of that particular brand of Christianity, and aspects of which he had come increasingly and painfully to question. It was to that sort of situation, and also from that sort of background, that he wrote. To transfer comments made under those circumstances to *all* religious ideas and practices seems to represent a serious failure both in imagination and in historical understanding – but it is a failure of which many contemporary writers are guilty.

Let us try to see some of the things that Bonhoeffer and others, too, such as Karl Barth in his celebrated attack on 'religion' in the *Kirchliche Dogmatik*, had in mind when they launched their criticisms and denounced what they took to be 'religious' attitudes, ideas, assumptions, practices.

In the first place, the conventionality of much popular, middle-class or bourgeois, piety was plainly in view. There can be no question that a good deal of church-going, much of the support of ecclesiastical institutions, and even some of the loyal participation in the life of 'the congregation' (as they styled it) in Germany – and elsewhere too – has been marked by a strong desire to associate with respectable people who are thought to be doing respectable things. In

Germany Bonhoeffer encountered a conservative sort of religion which had been so intimately identified with the *Reich* that it had lost its prophetic voice. In circles more familiar to us, there has been a tendency to think of religion as a support of 'the American way of life' or as 'the inspiring power in English democracy'. There has been a tragic identification of the ecclesiastical institution with 'the conservative party at prayer' or with the maintenance of the American 'dream' of equality for all in a society which as a matter of fact has granted opportunity only for a very few. Nice people, wishing to preserve things as they knew them, wishing also (even if unconsciously) to keep their own position of privilege, have supported the churches because these bodies seemed to them to represent the 'old ways' and to stand for the established conventions. Against this sort of respectability Bonhoeffer was in violent reaction, for he saw perfectly clearly that it had not been able to oppose the demonic National Socialist 'take-over' in his own land and, far from preserving the essential decencies of life, had consented to, even acquiesced in, the horrible evils which were so terrifying to a man with Bonhoeffer's discernment.

Furthermore, the way in which certain kinds of religion, especially as he found it in established German Lutheran circles, had centred attention on man's sin and weakness seemed to Bonhoeffer (in his own words) to be taking people at their moments of despair and futility and frustration; and on that weakness and sin building the entire Christian faith. An induced sense of man's wickedness, with its corollary in a feeling of sheer human impotence, was the point of departure for much of the preaching and teaching with which he had been familiar. I have written elsewhere of a story told me by a young Lutheran who had much the same experience. He said that in his childhood in a midwestern American town he had been the victim of a scandalous manipulation of his emotions. In the local Lutheran Church which he and his family dutifully and regularly attended, the pastor always preached on sin and its dreadful consequences. With remarkable skill the preacher awakened guilt-feelings as he talked of man's condition, dwelling on alienation from God, helplessness before temptation, the certainty of damnation by a just God. The boy was terrified every Sunday morning. Nor was he much relieved when the pastor devoted the final minutes of his sermon to giving the assurance that in spite of all this which he had so eloquently proclaimed, there was the possibility of divine forgiveness and the chance of divine acceptance if those who heard him would repent and trust unfailingly in the God whose justice was indeed tempered with mercy even towards the worst of sinners. My young friend said that the technique was obvious. First, get your congregation at its weakest point, make them feel utterly despairing, induce in them a sense of guilt which is artificially created; and then, on the authority of the gospel which the minister is commissioned to proclaim, assure the congregation that God, after all, is 'gracious' and will save from hellish punishment those who in despair beseech his pardon. The young man when he 'came of age' gave up Christianity.

Now there is just enough truth in what was being said by his pastor to make the enterprise sound plausible, perhaps even legitimate. Man *is* a sinner; men often *are* in despair. All of us need God's assurance of forgiveness and acceptance and the gospel of Jesus Christ provides just this. But the way in which it was done, with its skilful use of the techniques which would induce the emotions thought to be right under the circumstances, disgusted my friend. When he gave up Christianity, he said, he was giving up what seemed to him the most immoral kind of religion that the world has ever known. He thought that it was entirely wrong to produce, by such manipulation, feelings of depravity and lostness, presumably in order to be able *then* (*only then*) to assure one's hearers that after all God was gracious enough to accept wicked men – and men, mind you, whose sense of sinfulness was not aroused by contemplation of the sheer love of God in contrast to their own lovelessness, but rather by exaggeration and misrepresentation of the facts about human life.

It was against *this* sort of preaching of sin and redemption that Bonhoeffer was in revolt. He was in revolt not only because of his own sensibility but because he saw clearly that such preaching really made no sense, and nowadays had no enduring appeal, to the great majority of men and women with whom, both in prison and before, he was in intimate contact. He was also aware of the enormous psychological damage done by this sort of proclamation of the gospel. It was not that men are entirely good; it was not that they are not in defection from God's will. Bonhoeffer never denied the fact of sin and the sense of sin; on the contrary, he knew all about them. But it was his conviction that the gospel and the Christian faith which it awakens must be associated with the strongest and best points in human experience. He was rejecting an *artificially* induced sin-feeling, the awful method employed to awaken in men a sense of guilt, and the use of Christianity as a device to deliver men from a situation which the preacher himself had created in them, rather than a deliverance from their genuine personal awareness of imperfection and defection and from their deep sense of personal responsibility for alienation from God.

Bonhoeffer was also protesting against the notion that there is a certain sort of human being who is 'temperamentally' religious. Just as there are some men who have a peculiar gift for art or music or science, so (it has often been

75

thought) there are those who have a special gift for 'religion'. This suggests that the Christian faith is not for *all* men, whoever they are and wherever they are and whatever they are, but only for those who have a flair for 'religious' beliefs and ideals and practices. That there are such persons need not be doubted; whether they are any 'better' than other men is another question. In any event, Bonhoeffer was sure that those whom he called (unfortunately, we may say) 'saints' are in no different case from the ordinary run of people. It was for him a denial of the universality of the Christian gospel to assume that only *they* can be true disciples of Jesus Christ. Such a notion scandalized the mature Bonhoeffer – and rightly so.

It was Dean Inge, I think, who said on one occasion that the 'religious temperament' is not unlike the musical one; some people have it, others do not. That is true. But the problem which must be faced here is whether the possession of such a temperament is necessary to a Christian man or indeed to any man. Certainly it is important to discover just what constitutes that particular 'temperament'; is it a special sort of sensitivity? is it some awareness of a 'more' in human existence, beyond what is tangible, visible, audible? is it a peculiar sort of 'experience' which some do and some do not enjoy? But whatever it is, it does not in and of itself make a man a Christian nor does it establish in him the conditions necessary if he is to encounter Jesus Christ and his claims. In any event, if to be a Christian is to be different from one's fellows in some strange way such as this, the faith is *not* for all men everywhere and at all times; its catholicity is denied and in its place we have a very odd kind of predestination which is much more devastating in its results than anything that John Calvin ever proposed. Bonhoeffer, for his part, would accept no such view.

Again, Bonhoeffer was critical of pietism of any sort – not only the 'sin-redemption' type with which he personally was most familiar, but also those types of piety which make the 'religious life' a matter of the observance of rules and the engaging in various kinds of systematic devotional practices. He had his own view of the necessity of the *arcana* as he liked to describe the hidden disciplines of the Christian's life; in one of his books, *Life Together*, he has much to say about this sort of ordered Christian discipleship. But for him this emphasis on the *arcana* did not suggest a 'rule of life' piety in either its Catholic or its Protestant dress. He thought that there was in both of these types too much legalism, too much obedience to imposed dictates; and above all he distrusted what seemed to him the over-individualism of that kind of thing. He had written, as one of his first books, a study of the meaning of the Christian Church; unlike many German Lutherans he had a keen sense of religion as community or fellowship – a strictly individualistic piety was to him the denial of that strong sociality which the New Testament shows to have been part of the Christian reality from the very beginning. To put his criticism of the pietism that he disliked in terms more familiar to English readers, he had no use for the 'sacristy rat' or the solitary 'holy man'; and he had a fine contempt for those who thought that God can be encountered *only* in the accepted and conventional routines and habits of churchly life. Some of his most vigorous strictures in his *Letters from Prison* have to do with this subject.

Finally, Bonhoeffer was highly critical of the kind of institutionalism which he found, or thought he found, in ecclesiastical dignitaries in their most 'professional' moments. He was well acquainted with them; he was friendly with them; he could and did respect them. Above all, he was well aware of the necessity for some organized communal expression of the faith, since (as we have seen) he was keenly conscious of the need that Christian faith have its life in fellowship. But very likely because he had witnessed the spectacle of such ecclesiastical leaders succumbing to the Nazi threat, he seems to have had a distrust of the usual organizational patterns with which, as a German Lutheran, he was familiar in the various *landeskirchen* and in the over-all structure of the Lutheran Church of the realm. He was unable to *identify* Christian faith with the institution in that sense. We might say, translating this into our own terms, that membership on parochial church councils, local congregational boards, the holding of ecclesiastical office, and the like, as well as active service of a local parish in the capacity of churchwarden, sidesman, lay-preacher, etc., did not for him indicate the real meaning of loyal and active Christian discipleship. It was perfectly possible to participate in any of these activities and still be a Christian, of course; but to be a Christian need not imply that of necessity one must be engaged in any of them.

These, I take it, were the sort of thing against which Bonhoeffer was protesting when he made his famous remarks against 'religion'. He had something else in mind, too. This was the view that a certain metaphysical position was inevitably included in the Christian profession of faith. Here he showed his background in still another way. Evidently for him 'metaphysics' suggested the idealistic philosophy of much German thinking or (if not that) subscription to some other specific ontological view. With typical German thoroughness, he simply crossed 'metaphysics' off his list of *desiderata*. Evidently he did not see that his own position, such as he intimated in the very letters which he wrote, was itself an ontological affirmation – albeit one that was very different from the sort that he disliked. With all his perception and despite his remarkable sensitivity, he was apparently unconscious of the fact that to talk, as he did, of the 'beyond that is in our midst' is to talk willy-nilly in a metaphysical vein. I believe that in his attack on what he conceived to be 'metaphysics', in an all-inclusive sense, he was really attacking both the idealism which in much German theology was simply taken for granted and the other (not so consciously held) kind of metaphysics in which God is portrayed as *ens realissimum*, absolute being, unmoved Mover, arbitrary moral governor, etc., while man is so denigrated that he counts for little in the scheme of things, his freedom being largely illusory and his ability to make a significant contribution to the divine purpose reduced almost to nothing. One might suppose that if Bonhoeffer had lived to work out, in detail, the theological implications of his teaching about the 'helpless God', the God who suffers in and with his creation yet assures it of the victory of love, and the Christian necessity of taking one's stand with and beside that God – 'before God', yet 'as if he were not there' – he would have been led to a kind of ontological affirmation that would have been similar to the 'neo-classical theism' of a Schubert Ogden in the United States or a Peter Hamilton in Britain (I refer to the former's book *The Reality of God* and the latter's *The Living God and the Modern World*), both of whom work towards precisely such a conception of God through the influence of Whitehead, Hartshorne, and much existentialist discussion of man's stance in the world.

I have gone through this list of Bonhoeffer's 'negatives' in reliance upon the total *corpus* of his writings and with particular reference to the brief notes (found in his *Letters*) for a book that one day he thought he might write. My purpose in doing this has been to show that far too much of the time those who talk so readily of 'non-religious Christianity', with easy allusions to Bonhoeffer, say much that Bonhoeffer would not say – and which Karl Barth most certainly regards as a complete misreading of his own celebrated remarks. But we must now turn, positively, to some of the things which (as I see it) Bonhoeffer and Barth would defend. They might not wish to use the *word* 'religion' to describe these things, yet historically such things have been part of the meaning of that word. In any event, words do not matter so much as the significant truths they are employed to denote. If the reality is there, the word does not matter so much. Yet as a matter of common usage, even today, the word 'religion' *does* include these positive things; and if we do not wish to impoverish our language or if we find ourselves unable to think up a new and supposedly colourless term, we had better not discard the term 'religion' altogether. What is more, to do so would be to set up an almost insuperable barrier between Christian faith and the 'natural man', who *does* include in the word the points to which we shall now give our attention.

First, then, religion stands for an attitude of creatureliness in the presence of the universe. It suggests humility before the mystery of things. Bertrand Russell once criticized the instrumentalism of the American philosopher John Dewey, on the grounds that there was a certain 'cosmic impiety' about it. The phrase is Russell's own; what he meant was that in Dewey's thinking man and his affairs are so central that the sheer cosmic range of things is disregarded or forgotten. Whatever we may happen to think of Russell's own philosophy – one might better say, his various philosophies, since he has not continued long in the same position – and however just or unjust we may feel his judgement of Dewey's teaching, the phrase he uses is a suggestive one. 'Cosmic impiety' is the precise opposite of the attitude which the religious man takes towards the universe of which he is a part. The religious attitude, which in this context means the stance of man in his moments of sensitive recognition of his place in the scheme of things, means a profound awareness of the fact that before the illimitable mystery of the world man is but a speck of dust. However important a man may seem to be to himself, however valuable his actions, the religious attitude is tied up with the strange feeling that 'the sea is so great and my ship is so small' – to put it in words attributed to a Breton peasant. Indeed, there is nothing peculiarly 'religious', in the pejorative meaning of the word, in such an attitude and such an awareness; it is simply a matter of common-sense and the honest recognition of things as they are. For the Christian, of course, this sense of 'creatureliness', as von Hügel styled it, has a special quality, since it is experienced in the presence of God who created both man and the world into which man has been thrust or from which he has emerged. But the honest and perceptive non-Christian is just as conscious of his very apparent relative insignificance in the total pattern and of the need for an attitude of humility in the face of the cosmos.

This awareness may be related to the sense of wonder which poets and artists have felt in the presence of the mystery of nature and in the contemplation of human life. But it is not only the poets and the artists who have felt this. It is they who have *expressed* it in memorable words or in suggestive forms and patterns. One reason that their work speaks meaningfully to others is that they put in visible or audible fashion, and with more profound evocation of meaning, what every man, at least now and again, has experienced. It may be before some grand vista in nature; it may be in the face of one he loves; it may be as he looks, for the first time, at his new-born child. There is mystery here. We shall do well to recall once again the important distinction made by the French philosopher Gabriel Marcel, who speaks about *mysteries* and *problems*. Problems can be solved; that is the nature of a problem. Mysteries cannot be solved; they abide with us always, for they are the objective correlative of that subjective sense ot wonder at the sheer 'thereness' of the world and of human personality. The scientist and those who like him are greatly concerned with the explanation, so far as may be, of physical and psychological phenomena, are men who are confronted by problems for which quite properly they seek a solution. That is, they want to know what this or that particular event or thing is made up of, how it functions, how it fits into a more general pattern, and how it leads to this or that consequence. But they are also faced, like every other man, with the 'thereness' of what is and is coming to be; they cannot do other than accept this in the attitude which Wordsworth styled 'natural piety'. In the presence of such mystery, the appropriate response is that reverence of which Kant spoke when he said that in the contemplation of the heavens and of man's moral sense he was 'filled with awe' – and this wonder, in the presence of mystery, seems an indelible feature of human life.

As I was writing these words, I came across Dr F. H. Crick's recent little book of lectures in which the distinguished partner in the discovery of DNA attempted to set out his view of the world. As is well known, Dr Crick is a vigorous, not to say violent, opponent both of the Christian faith and of all religion as he understands it. Yet often the language which he uses about the physical and chemical base of life is language which might seem more appropriate to a man engaged in worship than one who is writing of strictly scientific experimentation and explanation. Although Dr Crick is confident that there is and can be no *religious* mystery, he speaks about *the world as a whole* and about 'nature' in a fashion very odd from one who thinks that everything may ultimately be reduced to a series of mathematical formulae of a complicated sort. Despite himself, Dr Crick seems aware of the real mystery in things and in the cosmos. Perhaps Bertrand Russell was not far from the truth when in a famous essay he related mathematics and mysticism and wrote of the feeling of wonder which is present in the contemplation of the 'perfection' and the 'beauty' of the higher mathematics. Maybe there is a 'thereness', although in this instance an 'ideal' one, in the very 'elegance' and 'wholeness' of mathematical explanation, above and beyond its problem-solving competence.

This kind of experience, of mystery which awakens wonder, points towards what in an earlier chapter I have described as the awareness of a transcendent dimension in life. I was not referring there to what might be called a specifically *religious* type of experience in the ordinary sense of that term; I was speaking of that sense of the 'more' which, as I see it, is an indelible feature of all human living. How we are to interpret the meaning of this awareness is another matter; what the 'more' really conveys is another matter too. To it the great religions of the world have something to say, each in its own way. But the fact of the transcendent dimension, and the awareness of it, is found everywhere (so I am convinced), whether in the primitive savage or in the sophisticated modern – the phrase sometimes used by the latter, 'there's more here than meets the eye', is most revealing. There is that 'more'; and the artist, as well as the sensitive man who is not himself an artist, will know what it is about. In the presence of that which is sublimely beautiful, for example, we find it. So also we find it in the scientist, even when he speaks (like Dr Crick) *malgré lui* as he senses the profundity of truth, of which he can grasp but a very little. The ordinary man or woman, experiencing the 'wonder' of love, feeling himself caught into a relationship with another human being, is touched by that 'dearest freshness' which Gerard Manley Hopkins found 'deep down things'. Such a man or woman knows well that the love of another person, and the other person who is loved, is for him much more than the physics, chemistry, biology, and psychology of the human organism with which he is in relation. There is mystery here; there is wonder; there is awareness of the transcendent dimension.

It is indeed difficult to phrase what we mean when we speak of this perennial experience of man. We are always in danger of trying to state it exhaustively, in our own little words; but we know that we fail. On the other hand, we are in equal danger of succumbing to the temptation to speak in vague, indeterminate, sometimes sentimental, language, as we struggle for words and cannot find them. Yet this sense is most profoundly real; and to deny it or explain it away seems inhuman as well as idiotic. Not even the most appalling living conditions, as when men and women and little children are compelled to exist in degrading surroundings and to feel their lives cheapened and vulgarized, can completely kill this sense of wonder at the transcendent. One recalls a popular poem of the earlier part of this century, Alfred Noyes's *The Barrel-Organ*, in which the poet speaks of that lighting-up of the face, brightening of the eye, feeling of some 'presence' (dare we name it so?), which for the apparently dull clerk or unimaginative shop-assistant makes life different, deeper, more wonderful – although from that moment of experience they, like the rest of us, must return to the 'light of common day' with its triviality, superficiality, cheapness, and vulgarity. And John Betjeman has said the same in his fine verse about two quite ordinary people, a man and a woman, having tea in a restaurant or tea-room, and just for the moment illuminated by an almost celestial radiance. Is this nonsense? Is it sentimental lying? I think not; I think it is the opening of a window into the depths of human existence in a world of strange glory – a revelation, if you will, of the supreme dynamic in that existence and that world.

We are often told that man is a 'rational being'; the famous definition which St Thomas Aquinas took over from Boethius is well known: 'an individual substance of a rational nature'. But however true it may be that man is marked by a capacity for rational thought, it seems to me much more important to see that he is possessed of *imagination*. I am not speaking of sentimental 'fancy' nor of 'day-dreaming'. By imagination I intend the capacity in man to grasp with the whole of his being, by rapport between him and what he is confronting, that which is not himself; I mean his ability to experience at levels deeper than mere sense-perception and deeper than rational awareness; I mean his empathetic identification with some 'other' which comes alive to him and with which he finds himself strangely 'at one'. Call it intuition, if you will; call it sensitive apprehension – whatever it may be called, there is in man an imaginative quality which enables him to see, to hear, to feel, what is not immediately and obviously present on the surface of things. Perhaps one of the sadly unfortunate aspects of our modern and rightful emphasis on technology and on strictly scientific methodology – to which we owe so much – is that there is often a disjunction or bifurcation in human life and human experience, so that what we might style a 'rationalistic' interpretation (in consequence of a technological attitude) of reality is regarded as what really matters, while the more poetic, imaginative (call it mytho-poeic, after the Greeks) interpretation is regarded as secondary and perhaps as insignificant. Yet as Whitehead (and others) will make clear to us, the fact is that the aesthetic

85

quality, the 'feeling-tone', the imaginative understanding, is equally if not more important than the strictly rationalistic, technological side of our experience. Sometimes one feels that modern young people are in a quite terrible 'bind', to use their own word. They have been taught to think that technological, scientific, rationalistic types of knowledge (and the performance which these demand) alone give us truth; yet in their own deep experience they are keenly aware of other things – they fall in love, they read novels and see plays, they visit art exhibitions, they sense the enormous vitalities which emerge from their depths, and in these ways they seem to live more really and to find both happiness and sadness or 'the tears of things'. Yet they may feel that these latter are ephemeral, episodic, epiphenomenal – in a word, not 'really real'. One can only be thankful that they *do* 'break out'; one rejoices that they insist, often in startling ways, that what they *feel* deeply is for them most certainly important. In this they are but asserting their manhood and claiming for themselves the privilege of being authentically human. In the same fashion, we may interpret the so-called 'existentialist revolt' as a vigorous protest against everything that would cramp, inhibit, or minimize the 'free spirit of man' as he engages himself, with profound imaginative out-reach, with others and with his world.

It is obvious enough that this imaginative capacity in human experience can easily be confused with sheer fantasy; for such a confusion there is nothing to be said. S. T. Coleridge correctly portrayed the centrality in human experience of imagination; but he also saw the danger of the phantasmagoric dreams. If the imagination is permitted to operate entirely without relationship to man's rational capacity, it can be most horribly perverse and lead to conclusions that are both silly and false. But then reason itself need not be taken to mean only 'logic-chopping'; it is not simply ratiocinative thought. Reason can be, I should say must be, understood as 'the reason of the whole personality' – *including* feeling-tones; as Keats said, 'we think on our pulses'. Here we are indebted to Paul Tillich, among others, for making it quite clear that the very word 'reason' is open to two interpretations; it can mean ratiocination, but it can also mean something much more profound, something that is akin to faith. Richard Kroner has written about 'the religious function of the imagination' and has suggested that the commitment or engagement of self which we call faith is indeed akin to reason in this imaginative sense. I believe that he is right, as are those existentialist thinkers who have spoken of the quality of 'subjective pathos' in all really deep human awareness, whether of the self or of other men or of the world. 'The heart has its reasons, which the "reason" does not know,' said Pascal; and even if we do not care to subscribe to the Pascalian way of distinguishing between *l'esprit de finesse* and *l'esprit geometrique*, we must listen to his insistence on that insight, intuition, imaginative perception, which is an inescapable element in all truly human awareness. Imaginative reason is not irrational; it is not *un-*reason. Rather, it is 'beyond' ratiocinative, technological, 'manipulative' reason, as it is also 'beyond' reason in the syllogistic or strictly logical sense.

It is this imaginative reason in man which drives him to seek meaning. This he is always doing; and here we touch on still another abiding factor in the 'religious' attitude or way. As I have argued, religion can suggest to us the human awareness of the 'more'; it can convey to us the importance of that imaginative quality which is akin to, perhaps identical with, 'faith'. It is also the 'meaning-seeking' aspect of life. Human beings want to see and know, so far as may be, the *sense* of things; they also want to *make sense* of what they see. This double search, as we might call it – to find meaning and to give meaning – is not confined to some odd and unusual human beings here or there; it is found universally in the story of the race. What does life mean? – *my* life, the life of the other man, the life of nature, the whatever-it-is that is in, through, with, under, beneath, above, and behind what I see and hear and touch and feel? The question is inescapable; it is profoundly *human*.

Nor does the ordinary person think that it is he and he alone who *projects* meaning on the world. He assumes that meaning is there to be found; and when I spoke about 'giving meaning' or 'making sense', I did not intend to suggest any projectionist theory. The 'giving meaning' or 'making sense' is rather a taking of the deliverances of deeply-felt human awarenesses and sensitivities and the reading of them as indicative of 'how things go' in the environing cosmos. In other words, the ordinary person believes that in some fashion he discovers, either in the world around him or in the depths of his personality, what is there to be discovered. When he sees meaning, it is not he who has put it on to an entirely indifferent and careless mechanical pattern; when he tries to 'make sense' of things, he is sure that there is a sense to be made of them and that his efforts to 'give meaning' have some genuine correspondence with how those things actually do 'go'. This is why a sharp dichotomy between 'subjectivity' and 'objectivity' cannot be set up by any thoughtful person. Whatever is known as objective is subjectively apprehended; whatever subjective awareness we possess in respect to *what matters* is in some relationship with things as they are – we are neither individualistic nor social solipsists and no ordinary person acts as if we were. It is only the ultra-sophisticated who talk in this manner; and of them it is fitting to say, with C. D.

88

Broad, that there are 'some theories so silly that only a very clever man could have thought them up'. Yet even the 'very clever man' has his moments of being authentically human; he cannot *live* in terms of his 'silly theories'. It is said that sometimes David Hume, after a prolonged period of philosophical reflection, would go to a tavern and play backgammon; in this way, doubtless, he restored his common sense after an exercise in philosophical thought which led him to a theoretical denial of what 'every man really knows'!

There are two questions with which 'every man' must wrestle. One of them is, 'What are things *really* like?' It is the question of meaning. The other question is, 'How do I, how do we, fit into them?' This is the question of 'salvation', if I may put it so. It is with both of these questions that man as the 'religious' animal he is, must deal, somehow or other, to his satisfaction or to his discomfiture. Especially in respect to the second question, I should claim that a person who does not bother about its importance has either ceased to be human and has sunk back into sheer animality, or has let himself be persuaded that immediate concerns are sufficient to engage all his time, or (most likely) is deluding himself about what most profoundly even if unconsciously is for him the question of all questions.

Of course the way in which people have dealt with the issue has differed from time to time, from culture to culture, even from person to person. That is to be expected. Nor do the modes of phrasing the issue remain the same; the big question of 'fitting in' may be put in most various forms, again depending on the time when, the place where, and the circumstances under which this or that man asks it. The untutored savage and the learned theologian, the 'man in the street', and the man in his study, will see the question in different ways and will seek the answer in different ways too. But the question of 'fitting in' is a constant in human experience; and here once again I cite Bertrand Russell, since from one point of view the whole of his life and the entire *corpus* of his writing represent a sustained and heart-rending effort to see how he and other men *do* 'fit in', even when the exercise is undertaken in terms of a world that, if not unfriendly to man, is certainly unconcerned with him.

Such considerations lead me to another factor with which religion may be taken to deal. I refer to human inquietude. The American essayist Henry David Thoreau wrote once about the 'quiet sense of desperation' which, as he thought, is present in every human life. Perhaps he put it too strongly. Yet there is a sense of 'dis-ease' which runs through our experience. Kierkegaard spoke of man's *angst;* Heidegger has written about *sorge* or 'care' . . . whatever we wish to call it, there is a 'dis-ease', an inquietude, a strange but persisting uneasiness, which all of us know even if we try to hide from it by hectic activity. The thing may not be sharply articulated but as a continuing motif it runs through the literature of all races of men and in one way or another indicates something deeply felt in these men. If this were not the case one would find it hard to explain why, from the Upanishads in India, through the Greek tragedies, down to Dante and Goethe and Dostoevski (to mention but a few instances), there is a continuing portrayal of such 'discontent'; it would also make it difficult to see why these and other classical statements speak so directly and so evocatively to readers in succeeding generations.

Furthermore, it must not be forgotten that often it is precisely in the moment when a man feels quite safely ensconced in his 'secularity' that this disquietude makes itself felt. Browning in *Bishop Blougram's Apology* speaks of this in words which while perhaps too familiar are still pertinent: 'Just when we're safest', he says, 'there's the sunset-torch, a fancy from a flower-bell, someone's death, a chorus-ending from Euripides' – and that is 'enough' to awaken doubts, fears, uncertainties; all these, and the inquietude, too, which drives us to question and puzzle and wonder. And finally, it drives us on to something very close to, if not (as I myself think it is) identical with, the religious awe in the presence of mystery in the world, in history, in human life, and in our own personal experience.

This dissatisfaction, as we may style it, leads men to seek their true fulfilment in that which is beyond their present possession. There is not only 'more' in the world than we can at any moment comprehend; there is also 'more' in every man than at this or that moment he knows himself to 'be'. He *desires*, he *yearns*, he *seeks*. He is 'becoming', on the way to himself. When Jean-Paul Sartre talks about the *pour-soi*, the projective enterprise which is the self redeemed from sheer *en-soi* or 'mass-humanity' (so we may call it), he is pointing towards that drive or urge in each man to claim his freedom, act upon it, and express himself towards whatever self-fulfilment is possible for him. We have already urged the central place which must be given to human desiring; not in spite of, but because of, the physical, chemical, and biological basis of such desiring, it is integrative of human personality. When an attempt is made, by others or by oneself, to suppress it, man's desiring breaks out in various ways, some of them devastating and terrible. What is needed by each of us is some mode of fulfilling desire which will be for the best good of human society as a whole as well as for the best good of the person himself – and it is here that religion speaks to men of a fulfilment of their projective self which is human and trans-human, grounded in the cosmos, part of the structure of things, and a manifestation of the dynamic drive for good which we call God.

I have not exhausted, by any means, the positive significance of religion. There are other important elements which might have been mentioned, such as the sense of communion with what is taken to be more than a strictly mortal and mundane reality. But perhaps enough has been said to show that the wholesale condemnation of 'religion' is more than premature; it is based upon a surprising failure to discriminate between good religion and bad religion. If a man does not have a good religion, doubtless he will have a bad one; but a religion, in the positive sense that I should wish to give the term, he must have and he does have, even when he thinks himself anti-religious and rejects not only the established religious faiths but all that he understands religion to connote. The high religions of the world, as they have been called, speak to human beings about something which is not alien to them and contrary to their experience. They speak to men who have the stuff of religion in them; this is why they make the appeal they do and why they seem to possess a surprising capacity to revive and make sense. That they have such an appeal and that they manifest a remarkable ability to 'come to life again' after their death has been announced is for me evidence that there is something in man and something in the world to which they bear witness. How they do this, with what conceptuality, in terms of which theological formulation, is another matter. Briefly one might say that man's awareness of significance and his recognition that he must live in terms of whatever-it-is that gives this significance are testimony to the enduring quality and the abiding vigour both of the religious vision and of the religious enabling which is universally present.

Finally, I must return to my stress on love as the key to our understanding of man. If by love we mean, as we should, both the ability to give and the capacity to receive from others that which they in their turn would give, then religion may be defined as an abiding disclosure of what love really is about. The sense of the 'more' or the transcendent dimension in man and the world; the awareness of mystery and the response to that mystery in wonder and reverence; the search for meaning and the urge to 'make sense' of existence; the quest for fulfilment which comes when somehow one 'fits in'; the disquietude which marks human life – all these find their final point in love. Robert Frost has written of our reaching out to grasp the world and understand it, and our finding (when we do that) that we close our arms in the embrace of a lover. This seems to me to be exactly what the witness of the ages demonstrates.

Popular songs tell us that 'all the world loves a lover'; somehow, it seems, the lover speaks of that which is felt by every man and woman, however each of us may fail in love. It is no accident that such songs make their continuing appeal; it is not to be wondered at that song-writers compose lyrics about love and that those songs win the response they do. To describe such songs as nothing but an invitation to sexual experience, taken in its crudest terms, is to fail to grasp the depths of human life and to fail also to see what sexual experience implies for man. Of course the lyrics to which I am referring speak about sex; the question we must ask ourselves is what sexuality in man denotes and connotes. About this I have had much to say in an earlier chapter. The giving of self to another self who gives, the mutuality and the tenderness, the physical expression of an urgent and profound personal yearning for fulfilment, are what sexuality is about. The man or woman who knows what it is to love understands something about human existence and about the cosmos in which that existence finds its place, which the cynical, and jaundiced, the 'spinster' type, and the puritanical prig simply refuse to see or reject because it would upset their tidy notions of morality or

93

conventional respectability. Love, Whitehead once said, 'is a little oblivious as to morals'; just so, because it is concerned with something much more basic to man than morals. This is not to commend immorality; it is only to say that any viable morality must be based on love rather than on artificially imposed and arbitrary ideas as to what is supposedly 'right' for people. In genuine love there will be 'control'; but it will be 'love-control', not divine fiat which has no relationship with the vitalities of human life and the more basic vitalities in the universe of which that life is both an expression and a disclosure.

Even when the lyrics about which I am speaking appear to talk in what some would style 'crude physical terms', let us have the insight to recognize that their real intention is to speak to, evoke, and further the mutuality and tenderness which *is* love-in-action. And let us note that such songs are never an invitation to rape, in which another person is used without regard for his or her response; on the contrary, they are invitations to love, in which the response of the other is sought and is believed or hoped to be there, awaiting the incitation and solicitation of him who is 'the first in loving'. Deep calls to, and is answered by, deep.

The history of religion in man's experience is the story of the discovery that the basic structure of the universe is not found in power but in persuasion. As Whitehead argued, man has begun his religious quest with the recognition of a void which he would fain fill. From this sense of God as present in the very 'absence' of visible purpose and meaning and strengthening in the immediacies of mortal mundane existence, he has gone on to see in God the 'enemy' who is against him, who threatens him, who exerts power over him. But in its final and great stage of achievement, the religious vision knows that God is (as Whitehead said) 'the companion' – and as companion God is 'pure unbounded

94

love'. In Christianity, dare we claim, this insight is confirmed in historical event, for the essence of Christian faith is the taking of Jesus Christ, Love 'en-manned' in genuinely human terms, 'as the disclosure in act of the divine nature and agency in the world' – so Whitehead; so also, I am convinced, the truth of the matter.

The transcendent dimension is love-in-action; the mystery which compels our wonder is the mystery of love; the search for meaning is answered by the disclosure of love as 'the only survival, the only meaning', in Thornton Wilder's closing words in *The Bridge of San Luis Rey;* the quest for fulfilment is satisfied in a love that takes all there is of a man and gives him the 'fitting in' which enables him to live nobly or at least to live with some dignity; the disquietude which all of us experience is met by the assurance that one is accepted, cared for, secure in the hands of a love that 'passeth all understanding'. Certainly there is a great mystery here. This is why teaching about human relationships in love, which supposes that all that matters is a series of techniques, always fails to get to the heart of the experience of loving. For love is not simply techniques. Nor is man's basic adjustment to the world in which he lives to be accomplished simply by increasing his technical competence, enlarging his knowledge, and equipping him with more factual data so that he may control more areas of nature. Love as it is known intimately and warmly in our human sharing is the symbol – the effective instrumental means – of a relationship grounded in what an older philosophy might have styled 'reality itself'. And religion, as an abiding element in human experience, is a mode of man's loving which reaches out, which penetrates through all else, so that what is finally embraced is (as Frost said) the world – or as a Christian would wish to put it, the cosmic Lover who is God himself. It is Love *che muove il sole e l'altre stelle;*

Love is the moving force which makes sheer power seem shoddy and cheap. Genuine religion, without which we simply cannot do, is the way in which human beings in response to pressures upon them, relate themselves in ever greater clarity and self-understanding but with ever deeper self-giving and receiving, to that which is highest and most profound: God the Lover who is the *prius* in all our loving and who is the *summum bonum* in all our desiring.

5. How Does Christian Faith Fit In?

HOW DOES the Christian faith fit into a society which is more and more 'secularized'? How does it speak to men if they are the sort of being that we have sketched? How does it relate to a world of the kind we have described? And how does it complete and correct religion, if religion be interpreted in the fashion we have suggested? Is it relevant in such a context? Does it have an enduring significance for modern man, as much as it had for his predecessors?

On some of these questions we have touched in our earlier discussion. But it is now time to make a more complete statement. For it is my conviction, shared with all who 'profess and call themselves Christian', that it *does* fit in, it *is* relevant, it *still* speaks to men or may speak to them, and it is *still* significant. But it is also my contention that the Christian faith is in need of very drastic re-conception, not in its disclosure of God and man as respectively cosmic Lover and creaturely lover, but in its ways of stating that disclosure and in the kind of emphasis which will point up the enacted truth which constitutes its gospel. In this chapter and in the succeeding one we shall concern ourselves with such matters. First we shall speak of the abiding reality of the Christian faith when it is seen in terms of the conceptuality which (in my judgement) can provide it a contemporary frame and setting. Then we shall say something about the kind of reconception which is necessary if that faith is to be in vital, and vitalizing, contact with our own age.

I have just mentioned 'the abiding reality of the Christian faith', but this must not be taken to imply that in this chapter I shall present a conspectus of that faith. My intention, rather, is to discuss six points, central in faith, which have a special significance in the relationship to our time and our need, about which I have spoken. The six points are these: (1) God and the world are related one to the other in an incarnational manner, in which each affects and is affected by the other; (2) the event of Jesus Christ is a vivid and focal expression or disclosure of this relationship, with consequences that are decisively important once that vivid and focal fact is taken with the most complete seriousness; (3) such a faith demands of those who accept it a free decision, and a subsequent series of lesser decisions, taken in all responsibility; they are the corollary of a free and responsible attitude towards the world and to our fellowmen and they entail obligations in respect to our total moral life, although they are in no sense to be read as a compulsive moralism; (4) the fulfilment of man is not only in some supposed hereafter but in his present existence where he can find both meaning and also empowering strength; (5) the worship of God, which is the attentive or consciously realized relationship available to men here and now, is far from being the contradiction of responsible action in the

98

world, but is a proper expression of such responsible action, so that work and worship, worship and work, are correlative and mutually involved in any genuinely Christian discipleship; and (6) as a result of what has gone before, the existence of the Christian man or woman is of such an order that one is precluded from adopting a next-worldly attitude to life but required to find God, as one is found of God, in the place and at the time where each one now *is*, where God has put him, and where (as Christian faith declares) God has also put himself.

When Christian faith has been true to the biblical pattern upon which it is based, it has always seen God and the world in a relationship of interpenetration. That is to say, it has refused to adopt a deistic picture of God as remote and unconcerned with the world, once it has been created. It has not talked of God as if he were aloof from his creation, intervening 'from outside' on particular occasions but most of the time allowing it to go its own way. On the other hand, it has not identified God and the world after the manner of pantheistic philosophies and some of the eastern religions. God and the world are distinct one from the other; they are not separated, however, for to say that would be to speak once again in the deistic fashion. Doubtless few Christian thinkers, in the so-called 'orthodox tradition', have been much tempted to succumb to the pantheistic fallacy, although there are elements of 'pantheism' (of a refined sort) in certain great theologians like Scotus Erigena. They have been much more tempted to think in a deistic way. Indeed, one might say that much which is commonly regarded as highly 'orthodox' Christian teaching is in fact nothing but a variation on the deistic theme.

The sort of talk about transcendence which suggests a God 'up there', almost spatially 'above' the world, is a case in point. Popular preaching and teaching often conveys just this impression. Poetical phrases like 'came down from heaven' are taken in a literal way, so that God is thought to 'enter' the world, as it were from another sphere where usually he dwells and to which he returns. We need not doubt that there are places in Scripture which might suggest such an idea. But it is obvious that such language is mythopoeic rather than literal; and the main direction of biblical thinking is towards a view of God as unfailingly present in his world; he does not need to 'enter' it, although he may intensify his activity in particular places and at particular times. But he is always *there*, or else (as William Temple used to say) the world itself would not be in existence at all. God is the creative source without whom, in biblical thought, there would be no world at all, since it is his sustaining power and presence which works to maintain the creation at every instant. Certainly in the main Jewish-Christian tradition, God is always taken to be related to the world in such a fashion that he never for a moment 'leaves it'; on the other hand, he does not interfere with it if this implies disregarding its ways and working against its created structures and dynamisms. He works in and through and with and by created things and persons and events.

Even when we read about what we call 'miracle' we must not think that this means occasional intrusions by God into the created order. Indeed, the word 'miracle' is hardly a biblical word and suggests to us ideas that have no real scriptural foundation. The concept of the miraculous has a different point. In another book I have discussed this question at length; perhaps I may refer the interested reader to what is said there (*God's Way With Men*, Hodder and Stoughton, London, 1969). For our present purpose it will suffice if I make only a few remarks on the subject. As we can readily see when we consider not only how the 'miracle-stories' are told in the gospels, for example, but also how they are 'used' by the evangelists (with what purpose, to what end), the point of them is that God is revealing himself for what he always is and what he is always up to. The given incidents may involve what we should describe as extraordinary occurrences, if not in the actual event itself then certainly in the telling about the event. God is represented as doing 'new things', but they are not the sheer contradiction of what his purpose has ever in view.

Furthermore, the words which are used in Scripture in presenting these occurrences help to make the intention clear. In the New Testament, for example, there are three terms employed for this purpose. 'Miracles' are said to be *signs* (*semeia*) in which God's goodness and love for his creation is revealed in given situations of human need. They release God's *power* (*dunamis*), making his good-will for his creation more effective, because more intensively operative, under particular circumstances. They are unexpected occurrences, wonderful or marvellous in their impact; hence they are called *terrhata* (wonderful or marvellous events). Something takes place which makes people 'sit up and take notice'; God's children are brought to see that in fact God *is* at work in his world – and 'it is marvellous in our eyes'.

But the Bible does not talk in terms of secondary causes, relatively ordered and settled, with which God interferes to indicate his presence, to reinforce his energetic working, or to cause men to stand in awe. The most certain way in which we shall *mis*-understand these stories is by taking them from the context of an almost immediate divine operation in the world, as the Jews saw it, and placing them in the context of our modern scientific world-view. The point and purpose of the stories is precisely what we have indicated; the outlandish science of the biblical writers does not diminish that significance. And it is a great mistake, theologically speaking, to permit oneself to be so bogged down in the details of the story and so intent upon demonstrating its probable historical character (or its probable non-historical basis), that we forget the reason the stories were told. Jews and early Christians lived when they did; their patterns of thought, scientifically speaking, were not ours. The writers inevitably put down from oral tradition the accounts they had received, setting them in the kind of view of nature which was theirs: how could they have done otherwise? The abiding *religious* significance of the miraculous is found in its testimony to the inexhaustible reality of the divine love, energizing in the creation, accomplishing the ends which God has in view, defeating all that seeks to go against that end, bringing to his children his gracious aid and his never-failing care.

God is always in and with his world, then; and whatever we may feel obliged to say or think about him apart from that world is based upon, as it must be congruous with, what we know of him through that relationship. I have called this an 'incarnational' view of God and the world. Of course I know that some recent 'biblical theologians', as they call themselves, have no use for this idea as a general principle which may thus be applied to the whole picture of God-world relationship. They say, correctly enough, that the word 'incarnational' is not to be found in Scripture. When I go on to say that such an incarnational view demands also that we think of the universe as a 'sacramental' one, they will become even more irritated. For they will say, again correctly, that they do not find that word, in that sense, in Scripture. But in each case they are utterly wrong, so far as *meaning* is concerned. The point is not whether or not those particular *words* are used. The point is that the scriptural portrayal of God in his relationship with the world, and of the world in its relationship to God, is of a certain sort. It is my conviction that the Bible portrays the divine reality continually and dynamically entering into, ceaselessly working through, unfailingly disclosing himself within, the realm of creaturely occasions which we call the world. The basic question which we must face is whether the way in which God is in fact found in that realm of creaturely occasions is of the order which may be described as 'with, in, and under' (to use again the appropriate words derived from Lutheran eucharistic theology) his creation, or whether it is of the order which can only be described as the entrance, 'from outside', of the divine reality into the creation – an entrance which if not contradicting or denying or minimizing the reality of the world, yet does signify that apart from such intrusive action God is separated from that world. If he is conceived, in relationship to the world, in the former fashion, I should insist that the words 'incarnational' and 'sacramental' are entirely appropriate, even if they do not happen to be found in the text of Scripture. After all, *homo-ousios* was adopted by the Council of Nicea as a way (under the circumstances of the time the *only* way) in which the biblical understanding of Jesus could be safeguarded – and the term is not in Scripture.

Professor Whitehead, in what seems to have been his last known utterance, said that 'God is in the world [or creation] or he is nowhere'. This seems to me an eminently sound remark. For what is the *where* in which God might be, if it is not the world? Whitehead's intention was not to deny that God is in a serious sense 'transcendent', for elsewhere he had his own way (which I for one find both illuminating and helpful) of securing that for which 'transcendence' stands. The question which we must face is how to understand the divine transcendence without making

God 'separate'. I suggest that in any sound theology, such as will make sense today, the term must be used in the following way. It indicates the inexhaustibility of the cosmic Love, the distinction which must be made between that Love and the realm of creaturely occasions in which it is ever at work, and the fact that the creation in which cosmic Love is now present is neither so confined nor so 'finished' that there are left no possibilities for the supreme Lover to express himself in new ways, with the use of new reserves of loving energy, and with a capacity to accomplish, in and through that world, his indefectible purpose of increasingly shared good. I believe that this is consonant with the main drive of the biblical view, much more so than a notion of transcendence which speaks of a static and untouchable perfection far above the created order.

So much for our first point. The second is an affirmation that in the ceaseless incarnational activity of God as he relates himself to the world and is open to affect from the world, the focal moment is the total event of Jesus Christ. This is the peculiar claim of Christian faith itself, which dares to proclaim that the relationship between the divine reality and the creaturely occasions has its definitive expression, so far as human existence is concerned, in a Man. It is in one of our own kind that God's nature and his manner of acting find their peculiar disclosure, so that they may be brought home to humanity. Dr J. H. Oldham once said that 'if we want to make a thing real we must make it local'. This is precisely what God has done in Jesus Christ: the divine Love now has 'a local habitation and a name'.

There have been theologies which have separated the world from God to such a degree that they have in consequence been obliged to regard Jesus Christ as an anomaly in what is essentially a 'Godless' world. I should argue that this is a shockingly unscriptural position. On the contrary I should say, far from being the supreme anomaly, Jesus Christ is 'the classical instance'. I use here a phrase that I have employed elsewhere; but I do not think it can be bettered, immodest as the claim may seem. Nor do I think that the *speciality* of Jesus is denied by its use; all that is denied is the tendency to make him irrelevant because unrelated to all the rest of God's activity in the creation. At any rate, there can be no real doubt that the mainstream of historical Christianity, in a different idiom of course but none the less certainly, has set Jesus Christ in the context of a continuing God-man relationship which he both crowns and illuminates. He gives sense to, because he makes sense in, a world which is *never* apart from, or without, God's presence and activity.

Yet honesty compels us to admit that classical christology has usually so interpreted Christ, even while maintaining (through its doctrine of the Eternal Word, or Second Person of the Trinity, who not only was 'made flesh' in Jesus but was also and always the agency 'by whom all things were made') the close relationship between its Lord and all God's action in the world, that the insistence on that intimate association can be made, theologically speaking, only with the greatest difficulty. To take one point as an illustration, the commonly taught notion that our Lord is 'utterly different in kind' from any and every other instance of God-world and God-man relationship, makes it almost impossible to speak of him in the way in which we should wish to do – and the way in which practical Christian faith in its deepest intentionality would seem to have to speak. If we think of Jesus as thus different in 'kind', it is hard to see how we can at the same time think of him as so much one with us, so much a man, so much involved in and so much part of the ongoing movement of divine penetration into the world and the responding human co-operation with God, that he is both the symbol of that double-movement and at the same time the signal and definitive moment in it. We need not question that the intention of those who speak of the 'kind' difference is to safeguard the 'signal and definitive' quality I have just mentioned; but the fact is that when one speaks in such a way one has made Jesus a stranger and an alien to our human situation and hence removed him from our midst. The 'signal and decisive' side has to be asserted, without question; we must find another way to do it, one which will not make him what I have called the supreme anomaly.

For these reasons, some of us would wish to push to the very limit the insistence on the humanity of Jesus, as well as his congruity with the total God-man relationship in what we have seen to be its double-movement. Further, we should agree heartily with the nineteenth century theologian who said that the meaning of the Incarnation is that God is known always under creaturely limitations since he has willed to reveal himself thus. At the same time, we should urge that the speciality of Jesus Christ – that which makes him decisive in the God-man relationship, as Christians believe – must be grounded in some more satisfactory conception than the 'orthodox' notion of 'difference in kind'. The speciality is an aspect of what Professor Moule has lately styled 'uniqueness of inclusion' rather than in a sheer or absolute 'uniqueness' which removes Jesus from the company of those whom he was willing, even eager, to call his 'brethren'.

I believe that such considerations demand a re-thinking of the christological question; in several books I myself have attempted, as have other contemporary theologians in their writings, precisely such a task. But the point which is here to be stressed is the placing of Jesus 'in context', rather than seeing him as entirely 'other' in respect to the God-man movement. One way in which this can be done is by using the concept of 'importance'. This Whiteheadian idea will assist us also in maintaining what one might describe as the tremendous consequences of the event of Christ.

As I have shown elsewhere, Whitehead introduced into his philosophy the concept of 'importance' as a way of stressing the patent fact that each of us – and *a fortiori* the philosophical interpreter of things – must take his stand on something – be it event or person – which he can usefully employ as his key-disclosure of the dynamic and structure of the world. Whitehead himself believed that the deep intuitions in human experience and the analysis of what it is to be a man will provide such a clue. This is true, I think; but it is not illegitimate to go further and select one particular instance of human experience as *the* clue *par excellence*. Indeed Whitehead seems to have done just this when in several places he spoke of Jesus or of 'the brief Galilean vision' or of the enactment in Jesus of 'persuasion' as more profoundly real than coercive power or moral righteousness, affirming that in these moments we have our most profound opening of the way the world is being made and what it is basically like. But we must now ask what constitutes something or someone as being thus 'important'.

I take it that a particular event, whether in the life of a given person or in the history of a nation or in the development of a cultural pattern or in the world in a more general sense, is 'important' when it provides us with some key to the on-going process as a whole. It is a summation of the past, it strikes us in the present with unusual impact, and it opens up possibilities for future growth in understanding which (apart from it) would not be available. This is not a purely 'subjective' matter, although inevitably it has its subjective aspect – we have already insisted that 'subjective' and 'objective' must go together. The 'important' occurrence or occasion is a complex event (like all events) which makes its impact upon us but which also awakens a quickening, deepening, enriching response. We may suggest a very simple illustration. The experience of meeting a great man, attending to what he says and does, permitting his influence to work upon one, responding to his extraordinary gifts, and the like, not only produces in us an awareness that here has been a significant moment in our own life. It can also provide us with the stimulus which will enable us to become better, finer, more dedicated persons. Above all, however, it gives us a clue for interpreting the whole of his activity, so that we are able to say that we 'know' him and his character in a fashion which apart from that specific encounter would have been quite impossible for us. Thus the 'important' is able to deepen our awareness and in consequence to bring about results in our own understanding; at the same time, since any occurrence in the world is such that the world (after it has happened) is a different world, there is an 'objective' quality which careful analysis is bound to recognize. Once the 'important' has occurred, things are *different* for we live in a world in which there is what Professor A. Seth Pringle-Pattison years ago styled 'continuity of process with the appearance of genuine novelty'.

The person of Jesus Christ, with what he accomplished, when these are set firmly in the context of the general relationship between God and the world, and especially the relationship between God and man, has this sort of 'importance'. Objectively, Jesus Christ was very much more than just 'another man'; none of us, indeed, is *just* 'another man'. But with Jesus there was a signal speciality which the disciples recognized and to which they made their remarkable response. Subjectively, in responding to him (in the love, reverence, and obedience which was first shown in the disciples' response) those who knew him in 'the days of his flesh', and those who know him today, are enabled to see more deeply into the nature of things, to come to a more profound awareness of the purpose of the divine-human relationship, and to be 'changed' in such a fashion that they become 'men in Christ'. For the movement of God manwards in *that* Man, coupled as it is with the response of man to God in *that* Man, opens to others the possibility of contact with God now characterized by *him* – in the Pauline phrase which we have just cited, it is a contact or relationship which is 'in Christ'. It is 'en-Christed', marked by the specific sort of love which was released among us in Jesus Christ himself. We might follow some other writers, in this instance 'devotional' writers, and speak of 'the Christ-life' which has been made available for men. It is through Christ that we come to understand ourselves, other men, the world; he becomes 'the master-light of all our seeing' and he is the centre of all that we think, say, and do. Here is a special relationship with God which works itself out in all areas of our human existence. It is not purely intellectual; it is deeply personal and greatly empowering. As we have said, *it makes a difference*.

To approach the christological question along these lines may seem very different from the older ways of coming to an interpretation of Jesus' person and work. But I do not believe that it is really very different from the intention of our fathers in the faith; rather, it seems to me to be identical with their concern, even if the way of stating the conclusion is by no means identical. In both cases, we have a process of encounter and evaluation. The approach that I have suggested will mean, of course, that in various respects the resultant statement will not be the same as that found in, say, the patristic formulations. But this is not an occasion for surprise. The Church Fathers handled the question in terms that were their own; why should we not do the same today?

This way of thinking may lead us, to take one example, to a radical revision of the significance of the Christian assertion that Jesus is 'final'. Yet it is surely true that the attempt to state that 'finality' – I should prefer to speak of the decisive importance of the event of Christ, since 'finality' is both an ambiguous and a misleading term – in the older idiom does not make much sense today. The pathetic spectacle of a great thinker like L. S. Thornton attempting to defend the *old* idiom in a quite new world-view ought to be a warning to us. We cannot manipulate or adjust such an idiom so that it will serve us. In an entirely different context, old notions become unintelligible; they are meaningless surds. But what is even worse, when they are placed in the new context they no longer accomplish what in the older situation they were intended to accomplish. The context in which an idea is used will largely determine the content that the notion includes; if we wish to say 'the same thing', in such a new context, we must find another way of saying it.

In summary we may say that it is central to Christian faith to believe that Jesus Christ is the focal point in the relationship between God and man; he is also the especially quickening and enabling point. We need to find some way in which we can affirm this today, without lapsing into incredibility or so presenting Jesus that he is only one among many very good men. I am sure that this can be done. Nor is there anything in modern thought which makes our claim impossible or absurd. It all depends upon how faithfully we maintain the reality in question, how ready we are to use our own patterns of thought in doing so, and how open we are to the inspiring influence, which theology calls 'grace', that Jesus both embodies and conveys. Above all, it depends upon our sensitivity to the society in which we live, its 'secularizing' characteristics, and the way in which the actual concrete present-day needs of men, as they seek what they would not call but what we must call their 'salvation', are met by the event of Jesus Christ.

If God is deeply involved in his world and if in Jesus Christ he manifests that involvement in a peculiarly vivid fashion, it must follow that Christian profession requires that his disciples shall also be responsibly active in the affairs of men and in the realm of creaturely occasions of which they are part. Christianity, so conceived, is no withdrawal from the world or from men; on the contrary, it is concerned with both, carrying with it enormous obligations and demanding decisions. This has nothing to do with what earlier I ventured to call 'compulsive moralism'. It is not the supposition that we should make men conform to our own patterns and prejudices as these have developed in a conventionally respectable society. Rather, it has to do with the release of the energy of love, which Christians necessarily take to be the deepest and the most powerful force in the world.

I have used the phrase 'responsibly active' in respect to our relationship with and our attitude to the secular world in which we find ourselves. Let us now try to spell out some of the implications of such responsible activity. Two of these demand attention. In the first place, it is required of the Church that it shall make very plain to all men that it is no escape-hatch into which those who profess Christian faith may retreat in order to hide from the facts of life. It is not a way of extricating oneself from the world and its worries. Despite the somewhat noisy comments of people like Malcolm Muggeridge, Christianity is not so 'spiritual' that it rejects the vitalities of modern secular existence. It is not, as he seems to think it should be, against sex, against self-expression, and against the 'materialism' of everyday life. We have already said much on these points; but it is of first importance that the Church, through its leaders and by the witness of its membership should make its positive attitude crystal-clear. The Church when it *is* the Church as Christ's people living in the world, is a society which is chiefly concerned to bring the love of God in Christ into the midst of the world's affairs and in that context to work for the widest possible sharing of that love by men and women of every rank and class and type. The corollary of this summons to the Church is the co-operation of its people with all who are working towards the ends of justice, understanding, and goodwill, whatever religious faith they may profess and even if they profess no religious faith at all. This may mean, as increasingly it seems to mean in many parts of the world, dialogue and sometimes definite association with communists. It may mean that in North America, Australasia, and Britain (to mention but three English-speaking areas), Christians will find themselves working side-by-side with those who describe themselves as 'humanists' as well as others who without giving themselves a label are concerned with the welfare of human society. Certainly it requires association with all manner of 'odd' people. The Lord himself was willing to be in the company of 'publicans and sinners'; need we, can we, doubt that he would welcome the opportunity to be also with good people, of whatever sort, who wish to bring justice and peace to their fellows? It is not easy to work with those who do not share, who perhaps deny, the faith by which we ourselves live. Yet that is required of us.

What is more – and here is my second implication – those who see both the world and the Christian's responsible activity in the world in the way for which I have argued, will also know that *God* is at work through these humanist, secularist, communist, and other agencies. He is at work under what we may call one or other of his incognitos. It is of supreme importance to recognize that God does not always choose to accomplish his purpose of love through those channels which we might think to be obviously his. The position we have been urging demands that we see God at work in all that is good, right, sound, true, honourable, just, beautiful, loving. *These* are his incognitos, chosen by God as appropriate in particular areas or for particular ends. Such acknowledgement is part of the affirmation that the universal Logos or Word of God, who was decisively incarnate in Jesus Christ, is the self-expression of God in the *whole* creation.

Thus we ought not to think of our Christian task as the introduction of others to a God whom they have not previously known and whom, save for our intervention, they would never meet. Our task is to give the name of Jesus Christ, the name of Love incarnate, to all those encounters which lie deep in human experience. It is to awaken a response to that Love, thus fulfilling, completing, correcting, and implementing the concerns of men with what is good and true and right and loving, wherever that concern manifests itself. To take this attitude requires of Christians both insight and courage; but nothing less can serve, once we have come to understand the breadth of the divine Charity and the universal reach of the Divine Activity which is that Charity in operation in creation.

The fourth big point necessarily follows. True human fulfilment is not something postponed to life-after-death in what we call 'heaven'; it has its beginnings here-and-now, in the actual existence which men know in this present life. Of course such fulfilment, such realization of the divinely-implanted and divinely-nurtured potentialities of human nature, will not be completely achieved in this our planetary existence. But it would be disloyal to the love of God released in Jesus Christ if we sought to do what unfortunately many think we wish to do: that is, put off to some imagined 'other-world' what we ought to be achieving in this one. For after all, this is where God has put us; and we have no reason to assume that the present world, our present existence, is to be interpreted as nothing more than a waiting-room or ante-chamber for some future life 'out of this world'. *Where we are* has its own values and purposes, it offers its own opportunities of accomplishment; and it is surely a consequence of taking with utmost seriousness the incarnating and reconciling work of God in Christ to say that here and now we must begin to help ourselves and others to find at least partial fulfilment in accordance with the divine purpose for us.

Each man's fulfilment will be according to his own particular potentiality. As Baron von Hügel liked to say, every one of us has his own *attrait*, his special way of being drawn to God and hence of realizing his own possibilities in him. The rich variety of human personality requires this; there is no standard pattern of fulfilment to which everyone must conform. To call Jesus 'the Pattern', as Kierkegaard was accustomed to do, is not to suppose that he is to be imitated in every detail. What matters is the 'Spirit of Jesus'. This was naturally spoken through the special conditions of the first century, in a small Semitic country, with the particularities that such location requires. But what it *means* is the filial obedience in utter self-giving, the realization that in the divine will is our peace, as Dante saw, and also our true 'satisfaction' as we live in love one with another and *in* the Love which is God. Thus 'the imitation of Christ', in à Kempis's phrase, is not the copying of Jesus as a Jew of the first century, with the reproduction of those details that were appropriate to such an historical occurrence. To be Jesus' disciple does not imply that we are to do today exactly what he did in his own time. Rather, it is that we open ourselves to the basic energy that flowed through Jesus' life, permitting ourselves to be grasped by it and used of it. Our decisions and our actions will not be identical with his; but the quality of his life and the love which motivated him will also be alive in us. Thus, and thus only, is God's will done in succeeding generations; and thus only can each son of man come to the intended fulfilment of himself, beginning here and finding its completion in 'what God has prepared for them that love him'.

This brings us to the fifth point, the relation of worship and work. Here little need be said that has not already been implied, for it is or ought to be obvious that worship cannot be separated from life. We do not seek refuge in the sanctuary from the 'changes and chances' of this mortal existence. The Benedictine motto, *orare est laborare*, with its equally proper converse, *laborare est orare*, sets us free from any such erroneous disjunction. True Christian worship is both disinterested *and* 'involved' in the world's affairs. When we come together to worship God in Christ, we are responding with all our being to the call of love upon us; on the other hand, to worship is to be 'sent out', to 'go forth', into the world, to work for that love and to be enabled to do so by the 'grace' which worship provides. *Ite missa est*, the Roman mass used to end: 'Go, you are sent forth.' It is not that we worship only in order to find strength to work. The position is quite different. We worship *and* we work, we work *and* we worship; they are both of them the 'service of God' and it is not possible to give either the priority. Some have said that worship is the more important; but surely that overlooks the Johannine insistence that 'my Father worketh hitherto and still works . . .'

If *God* works in his world, those who are caught up in his purposes as what Whitehead called 'co-creators with him' (or, in Pauline idiom, as 'fellow-workers with God'), are not to put such action in a secondary place.

Modern revisions of the eucharistic liturgy have as one of their main objectives the plain expression of this basic Christian truth of the polarity of worship and work, adoration and action. God is present and active in his creation, they teach us; the words which are used are intended to make this abundantly clear. And the corollary is that God's people are to be participant in that activity: this also they intend to make clear. Nor is this double intention some peculiarly modern notion, for any student of early Christian forms of worship knows that from the very first days of the Church the world was brought straight into the act of worship and the worshipper was sent out to work in that world, because our Christian fathers in faith knew that it was *there* that God was to be served and it was *there* that his children were required to 'work together' with him in the effecting of his will. God gave his Son, not for the Church, but for the *world*.

Finally, as our sixth big emphasis in this chapter, the very existence of the Christian is *in the world*. By definition of his faith, this must be so. Hence no Christian can adopt towards God what might be styled an 'other-worldly attitude' (although the term usually has a different, equally mistaken, connotation). Certainly there is a duality about the Christian life, in that it hints at *more* than this world can give or can take away. The quality of that life, in its duel aspects, is stated for us in the New Testament when it speaks of *eternal* life – but this does not mean something merely in the future; it means something apprehended and known today.

The French religious writer Père Jean de Caussade insisted, in one of his discussions of Christian prayer, that we are to find God 'in the sacrament of the present moment'. That is, we are to find him when we are confronted with the demands of life, given the opportunity to make our response to those demands, and enabled to labour responsibly for God in the place where we are. De Caussade added that if we do not find God in this way, we shall not find him at all. We are to 'abandon ourselves', he said, to 'divine providence' in the place where it has put us. So, only so, can we know God as the one with whom we are in communion. Now we may not like the language in which the French writer made his observation; but the truth of what he said would seem to be inescapable. One of the perennial temptations for religious people, as we remarked earlier in this book, is to attempt to be more 'spiritual' than God himself, rather than to be as starkly 'materialistic' as God is. He does not disdain the world; he is in it, he works through it, he cares for it. When de Caussade spoke as he did he was simply insisting that we, like God, are *in the world* and that it is there that God and man have their meeting. Hence a positive attitude towards that worldly existence is required of us, rather than a negative or a hesitant one. Our very redemption depended upon *God's* taking and continuing to take such a positive attitude towards his creation. Are *we* to be different?

Notice, too, that the world in which God and man have their meeting is the world as it is, not as it might be or as some idealistically minded people would prefer it to be. It is the actual situation, just as we know it; it is the 'secularized' society in which we now dwell and of which, whether we like it or dislike it, we are a part. Everything that has been said in the opening sections of this book has its relevance here, for unless we presume to think that God is a sheer incompetent we must agree that *his* hand has been one of the causes in bringing about the situation in which we find ourselves and the 'secularization' of society which we see proceeding day by day. God may not be the *only* cause; indeed, he cannot be that, since the realm of creaturely occasions, in its freedom, acts too. But he is the 'sovereign ruler', in the sense that he uses other causes, respecting their freedom but moulding them in the end towards his own good purposes. The Christian faith 'fits in' with all this, helps to make sense of it all, and provides a loyalty for those who can accept it. It does this, not by sneering at what is happening in the world and in human society, not by seeking to contract out of that happening, but by acceptance of it in the confidence that 'in the sacrament of the present moment', through 'abandonment to divine providence' there at work, *God* is met. And the God who is met is the cosmic Love which was given human embodiment in the Man Jesus. *That* is the clue or key; *that* is why Christians can live in high courage, even in times which seem so badly 'out of joint'.

It is necessary to say these things, and to say them often, because it seems an inveterate habit of religiously minded people to regard their faith, as well as the worship in which rightly they engage, as un-related to the world and separate from its secular interests. If St Paul was perceptive enough to recognize that the 'men of Athens' despite their idolatry were in fact 'very religious' (in a *good* sense), we today must be realistic enough to see that much of the time we give to others the impression that we are 'too religious' (in a *bad* sense) – 'religious' in the escapist meaning of the word. One of the reasons the faith which we profess lacks appeal to our non-believing contemporaries, even when they are men of good-will, is that they find that our faith removes us from, rather than sends us into, the hurly-burly of life. To the degree that we merit their criticism, we are in apostasy

118

from the gospel and we deny in attitude and in act what it is of the essence of Christian faith to affirm with vigour and strong conviction – what, having affirmed, that same faith should drive us to be and to do.

So I conclude this chapter by repeating that the Christian, by virtue of his profession, must be a *worldly man*. He is not worldly in the vulgar sense of that adjective, which suggests shoddiness, cheapness, satisfaction with superficial pleasures, easy, self-indulgent living. He is worldly in that he finds his place and does his work in the world and in 'secularized' society, which is exactly where he stands as a man. If ever we hope to win our contemporaries to the faith which we accept, this must be made very clear.

Despite the chatter of people like Mr Muggeridge, who by their own confession are attracted to, 'enchanted by', the idea of the Incarnation, yet do not see what it *means*, we must reject 'spiritual religion' precisely because we *do* believe in the Incarnation – or better, in him who is the incarnate Lord. Most of our friends reject altogether an ultra-'spiritual' version of life, even if they toy now and again with eastern mysticisms and escapist routines. They reject such a version of life because, in spite of themselves and in ignorance of their historical background, they are yet the inheritors of the biblical and Christian view that we are put into this world to live like men, serving whatever earthly truth we know and doing whatever earthly good we can do. It is not only this pragmatic consideration which should move us, however. Much more important than the apologetic value of a Christian proclamation that stresses this world, there is the deeply theological necessity for such a proclamation. The faith is here at stake. It is integral to that faith to speak in this way; it is an inescapable consequence of the faith to act in this way.

I have asked the question: how does Christian faith 'fit

in' with the world in its present situation and with the society in which the process of 'secularization' goes on? I have answered it so far as I was able. Now I add that it is largely through the influence of Christian faith that 'secularization' has come about. Christian faith, building on the biblical portrayal of God and his world, has established the relative independence, hence the freedom and responsibility, of the created order. Yet it has done this without denying the pre-eminence and priority of God, in it all and through it all. Taken in its integrity, the Christian faith has taught that we have our existence in the here-and-now, in a situation which recognizes and values its own contribution to God's on-going achievement. At the same time, it is Christian faith which is able to give sense to, and make sense of, this secularity and the demands which secularity imposes on us. It is able to do this because it values this world, seeing it as basically God's world as well as ours.

For my part I believe that a Church which is vibrant with the love of God and hence with a love of the world which God has made, is making, and continues to make, will be a Church which is loyal to its gospel, true to its faith, alert and ready to serve God where he has deigned to let himself be served – in this present existence, in this world, in society. The last verse of Laurence Housman's hymn makes the point well:

> How shall we love thee, holy hidden Being,
>   If we love not the world which thou hast made?
> O give us brother-love for better seeing
>   Thy Word made flesh and in a manger laid.

The verse closes, as do all the verses of the hymn, with a prayer which is both the result of its previous affirmation and an invitation to action:

> Thy kingdom come, O God, thy will be done.

6. Can We Re-conceive Christian Faith Today?

T H E S H O R T answer to the question which forms the title of this closing chapter is: 'Yes, we can and we must.' In the preceding discussion, especially in the last chapter, we have intimated some of the ways in which such re-conception may proceed. But that it is necessary would appear to be beyond doubt; and that it is possible is not only a matter of faith – in that no Christian can for a moment think that his faith is incapable of meeting the needs of men in every age – but a matter of course, as I might put it. By this I mean that it is of the very nature of the Christian enterprise to be open to such re-construction, indeed to invite it. For the essential Christian reality is a dynamic process and not a static set of ideas. The words which the Fourth Gospel puts in Jesus' mouth are significant: 'He [the Spirit] shall lead you into all truth, for he shall not speak of himself, but he shall take of mine and declare it unto you.' The energizing Spirit released in Jesus Christ releases us too.

It is also true that the development of modern thinking, in its scientific and philosophical aspects as well as in other respects, makes available to us an enormous amount of material which may be used for re-conception. Although many seem to mourn the 'loss of faith' and feel that the whole trend of modern thinking is *against* Christian conviction, it is my own belief that precisely the contrary is the case. What has happened, I believe, is that we have been delivered from a great many notions which made Christianity seem absurd. Our modern situation and the very 'secularization' which so many decry appears to me to provide extraordinary opportunity for the re-conception which is so necessary. We may find ourselves forced to believe 'less', in the sense that excess luggage must be discarded; I think that we shall also find ourselves able to believe 'more', in the sense that the 'things which cannot be shaken' will stand firm and will demonstrate their capacity to be put much more effectively in terms of the new patterns which contemporary science, a good deal of modern philosophical thought, and the unitary world-culture which we now must accept, make available to us.

In this discussion I shall concentrate on four points which seem to me to be of major significance. They are: (1) the working-out of a processive or developmental view of Christian faith itself; (2) the changes in our understanding of worship and prayer; (3) the substitution of a 'situational' ethic of love for a view of morality in which man's ethical responsibility has been seen as obedience to laws or commandments or codes, supposedly enunciated once-for-all in a set of propositions; and (4) the inevitable expression of Christian discipleship in social action as well as in personal life, so that the supposed gap between religion and life, the 'sacred' and the 'secular', (or in old-fashioned language, the 'supernatural' and the 'natural') is seen to be the monstrous

122

lie that so many of our contemporaries rightly think it to be.

Each of these points should have our most careful attention. I am confident that a serious reckoning with them will provide for us at least some of the theoretical background we need if we are to make much progress. Without such a theoretical – theological, if you like – background, a good deal of our practical activity will be inane and ineffective. George Tyrrell once spoke scathingly of those who 'think that Christianity is going about doing good, especially the kind of doing good which requires a great deal of going about.' Perhaps that was unduly cynical; yet the saying has its truth. Activity without purpose, efforts at re-conception without theoretical as well as practical justification, can be frustrating and fruitless. The person who is simply and solely an 'activist' is rather pathetic; he reminds one of George Santayana's pointed definition of a fanatic: 'a person who re-doubles his effort when he has forgotten his aim.'

In view of what has been said earlier, it is apparent that I am not for one moment advocating quietism in place of 'activism'. I am urging only that there must be a purpose and direction, a theoretical understanding and the use of a sound conceptuality, which will give value to what is being done, whether this is in the realm of practical affairs or in the area now our concern – the task of re-conceiving the faith which we have inherited and which we accept as true. Men and women soon weary of *doing* things when they have no idea why they are doing them and no goal towards which they are working.

I begin with the business of working out a processive or developmental view of Christian faith. When it has been true to its own nature, Christianity has always been a vital movement, what I have called a 'process'. This dynamic quality is observable in the early days of the Church; it manifests itself from time to time in such revivals as Franciscan spirituality or the Methodist movement; it is often seen, even within our own memory, in the so-called 'missionary areas'. Yet we are familiar with the conventional notion that Christianity is essentially a set of ideas or beliefs which have been established once-for-all and which it is our duty to hand on unchanged to the next generation. In the Roman Catholic Church today the opposition to the 'progressives' has been associated with just such an idea of the nature of Christianity. The pejorative term often used for this is 'triumphalism', a word which means that the theological positions reached in the past, as well as the whole ethos of ecclesiastical life, represent the final, accurate, and utterly unchangeable statement of the faith and all that follows from the faith. Now there remains only the duty to defend the positions which have been reached. But not only among our Roman Catholic brethren is this 'triumphalism' found. In the 'Reformed Churches', whatever they may be called, much of the same spirit often prevails; there are those who cannot conceive of the possibility of change, growth, or development. For them, it is all *fixed*, established and set.

I should be the last person to wish to claim that there is nothing firmly established in Christianity. To say that would be to say that Christianity means nothing in particular; it would suggest that Christianity is nothing more than a reflection of ideas and practices which at any given time happen to be popular or seem to be useful to those who may wish, for some reason, to call themselves by the Christian name. But what is permanent is surely nothing other than Jesus Christ himself and the disclosure in act of God through him, with its corollary in the disclosure of man's nature too. The various theories and theologies

124

which have been devised to explain and to communicate this permanent Christian *thing* are not in themselves unchangeable, however, nor are the practices which follow from it and the ways in which it has expressed itself in particular circumstances. Indeed, they *must* be modified from time to time if the central affirmation ('the gospel', as we Christians call it) is to be communicated to men and women who in each age live in different circumstances and in a world that is by no means identical with that of their ancestors. So also with the explanations of what this Christian 'thing' has to say to people in each new time and place. These must always be in terms which speak directly to those for whom the explanations are being provided. An explanation which does not mean anything to those who are being addressed is no explanation at all; it simply makes more difficult the comprehension of the faith and what the faith is about. Just here is one of our problems today. A good deal of our theology, as well as the frame of mind with which that theology is often associated, seems to the vast majority of our contemporaries to be related to an earlier, and for them incomprehensible, worldview.

Surely this Christian faith is a dynamic, living thing. The reality of God's love, declared in act in the Man Christ Jesus, with the consequences of that act in human experience, do indeed stand secure. But this does not preclude the continuing self-expression of God in the affairs of his world, nor does it suggest that his revelation in Jesus is to be conceived as exhausting the divine creative activity. There is always 'more truth and light to break forth from God's holy Word', as the Pilgrim pastor John Robinson is reported to have said. Nor is the Word confined to Jesus himself; it is defined by him for what it is and for what it does to accomplish a renewal in the lives of men and in the occasions which constitute the created world. Thus we are

125

given both a stance from which to proceed and a drive to go forward; we are permitted to know God in the distinctive Christ-event, yet we are also impelled to open ourselves to the unceasing activity of that same God as he continues to work in his world – to work, let us remember, in the manner and mode of incarnating action, bringing his children to himself, granting them the fulfilment of personality in community with their brethren, and establishing his purpose of love in his creation. This way of understanding the Christian faith enables us to be alert to new disclosures, which themselves will throw light on the central figure of that faith, and invites us to see new occasions in which the unchanging love that is God operates in us and for us, with us and by us, in the created order. God is always there; he never absents himself from it nor does he cease to labour to accomplish the good which he intends for it.

The Epistle to the Ephesians, whoever may have been its author, gives us the New Testament charter for a conception of Christianity as a living and vitalizing process. It sees Jesus Christ as being 'fulfilled' in the Christian fellowship, the Church, in which his presence and his work are carried on through those who are his members. The historical event of Jesus Christ is not put in isolation from the men and women who are incorporated into him by baptism; on the contrary, the Church, in this profound interpretation of its significance, is 'the fulness of him that filleth all in all'. Further, the Church (thus understood) is itself not in isolation from the world; it is the earnest or spear-head of the whole race of men, indeed the whole cosmos, which in due time will come to make its response to the divine Love and hence will be the adequate sphere for the divine self-disclosure. The race of men, coming to a focus in the Man Christ Jesus, is the point of penetration, but not the only point, in God's ongoing fulfilment of his purpose in the created order. The whole tractate, which we miscall an 'epistle', is a remarkably beautiful and clear presentation of an organic and processive conception of Christianity.

If there is any problem about the Ephesian author's discussion, it is in the difficulty many of us feel with identifying the Church as he portrays it with the ecclesiastical institution we know. Yet the writer makes provision even for this, since he urges that the membership of the Church, indeed the fellowship with which he was himself familiar, is to 'grow up' into the true Church which is Christ's Body. It is the true Church which is 'without spot or wrinkle', not (evidently) the observable empirical institution. Yet he refuses to make a sharp disjunction between the two. Perhaps he was wiser, possessed of more insight, than we are today; maybe we can learn from him that even in the conventional and shoddy institution we *call* 'the Church' there is the hidden presence of the actual Church – not the 'ideal' Church, mind you, for to talk in that fashion would be to succumb to a specious platonizing which would falsify the New Testament picture. In any event, we have in Ephesians a dynamic and vital view of Christianity, very different from the mechanical and static picture which so often seems to dominate the thinking of those who call themselves by the Christian name.

If something like this is the truth of the matter, so far as Christian faith and the Church's existence are concerned, we must go on to recognize that our apprehension of the significance of worship and prayer must also be along dynamic lines. This brings us to the second point in the present chapter.

The way in which most of us think about prayer and worship is 'conditioned' by the sort of general world-view in which we have been brought up. This is inevitable; but it means also that those who are outside the charmed circle of Christian faith will necessarily read prayer and worship in precisely the same terms. We need to let our understanding be corrected, not only by the biblical presentation of these matters, but also by setting them in the context of the dynamic process which *is* the world as today we know it to be. Our own general world-view, whatever may have been the picture we learned in our youth, must be made consonant with the modern one – this is no mechanical universe, neither is it one in which there is simply a re-shuffling of 'stuff'; it is a living, changing, developing universe. I think that while most of us may accept this in principle, we do not apply it to our thinking about prayer and worship. These are still conceived in terms of inherited notions and because this is so, the activity of worship and the practice of prayer seem utterly remote from the ordinary affairs of daily life and the social patterns which dominate society. For this reason it is no wonder that our contemporaries find such activity quite meaningless. If the truth were to be told, many Christians are in the same situation. They may continue to pray and they may still 'go to church' to engage in worship. But as a matter of fact, they find prayer and worship very nearly senseless. In a 'secularized' society, set in an expanding cosmos, in a world in which we no longer put the responsibility or the blame on God for what we know perfectly well is our own responsibility and our own fault, in a world which (in Bonhoeffer's famous words) is 'come of age', much that goes by the name of prayer or of worship is worse than irrelevant – it is absurd. Prayer conceived as a subtle device for getting God to do what we should be doing but are not inclined to do cannot be defended. Worship as an escape from engagement in the world's affairs is in the same case. Neither of these will make sense; both of them will seem a wicked refusal of our human duty in the places where we are put to live and to work.

I shall not attempt here to spell out the changes in attitude and the revisions in practice which are required in our new situation. I content myself with saying that in my own experience I have found that such books as Teilhard de Chardin's *Le Milieu Divin* are enormously helpful in making the adjustment which is demanded of us; and I can testify that many young men and women, for whom prayer and worship had become meaningless exercises which they continued only because they thought it to be their 'Christian duty', have been enabled once again *really* to pray, but in a new fashion, and really to worship, but with a different understanding, once they have read Teilhard and some others. We may be grateful that a few writers are now producing books to help us along these lines; and we may be even more grateful that liturgical revision is now tending in the same direction. Without such work, the whole enterprise of communion with God through personal prayer and public worship will become less and less a viable possibility for contemporary Christians, while for those outside it will appear an idiotic business. Tinkering will not serve; what is required is radical change. I have seen people's capacity for prayer effectively implemented after a reading of Teilhard and (for another example) Quoist's little book of modern 'spirituality'. And I have observed that a congragation of Christian people comes to a new and vivid realization of Christian worship, when they have the chance to engage in it with the use of (again to give but one example familiar to me) the revised communion service in the Church of England.

The third area in which reconception is now taking place is found in the moral life – which is to say, in the human making of decisions and in the human action which follows such decisions. The change is already having its results, not always to the liking of some in official or quasi-official quarters. In a world like ours and in the context of a 'secularized' society, the only possible moral pattern is the type often called 'situational ethics'. I do not wish to defend any particular statement of this newer ethical position, but it is increasingly plain that code-morality can no longer serve us. Something must come in its place; and what is coming is the approach which I have indicated by the perhaps doubtful phrase used by many writers: 'situational ethics'. Here we have the substitution, for unworkable code-morality, of an ethic based on love and finding its expression in given situations as these provide opportunity for the 'doing' of love under particular conditions and in the light of particular necessities.

Something of this sort has always been present in Christian moral thinking, although it has been smothered by the persistent notion that morality is essentially a matter of obedience to the supposed dictates of God. These dictates may have been regarded as handed-down from on high, like the Ten Commandments; or they have been seen as necessary implicates of 'natural law'. In any event, they have been presented as demanding undeviating obedience precisely because they are entirely divine in origin and are the direct communication of God's will to his creatures. The changing of our view of the nature of revelation, quite as much as the concrete situations in which we find ourselves, renders any such notion intolerable. It is not in this way that God communicates his purposes to men. He does not speak 'from Mount Sinai', neither does he give us detailed directions through some presumed 'natural law' – although what is said in codes may very well reflect valuable moral insight and what is deduced from man's rational understanding and his recognition that 'the good is to be done and the evil avoided' may provide useful 'guide-lines' for ethical decision. But if God does not reveal himself through propositions nor indicate his will by the announcement of moral dictates, the meaning of the moral life must be sought in another way. We know this and we accept it most of the time, at least in what might be called our 'non-religious moments' – that is, in the ordinary decisions required of us in daily life, in social and economic and industrial and national and international affairs. Yet in the specifically 'religious' context we tend to forget what we know and what we accept in other contexts; especially, in questions of what is styled 'personal morality' (above all in sexual matters), the old notion still lingers on. Hence our difficulty today in expounding, let alone commending, a possible Christian morality both for ourselves and for our contemporaries. Hence also the apparent irrelevance of the Christian moral pattern in a world which neither comprehends nor appreciates what those of us who are within the Christian churches are trying to say.

In many circles within the churches the advocacy of what I have called (following Professor Joseph Fletcher's usage) 'situational ethics' is often regarded as an invitation to utter laxity and permissiveness about the moral life. The presentation of 'ethics without rule' seems to them to be the presentation of no ethics at all. But this is a silly position. The question which should first be asked is: what do we *mean* by ethics? – or better, what do we *mean* by morality? For a Christian, one would think, ethics or morality means a style or pattern of human life, individually (I should rather say, personally) and socially. No particular details are implied in the first instance. What *is* (not implied but) required for the Christian is a style or pattern in which love, such as was manifest in Jesus Christ, is the key. But love is different from law; law is a series of enactments or

131

duties which relate to this or that instance, while love is an attitude of mind and heart and will, a way of seeing and of doing, which in given situations and in particular contexts is to express itself. Surely this ought to be obvious to everyone, above all to the Christian.

Nor is the change from a law-ethic to a love-ethic a change from high standards to low ones or to no standards at all. As a matter of fact, it could be argued that an ethic which insists that so far as may be possible we must live in terms of love's commands and love's demands is one which requires from men *much more* than is asked from them when their moral life is defined in commandments or codes or laws that were handed down once-for-all in the remote past. Surely it is more exacting to attempt to do 'the loving thing' in each and every situation, than to follow a specific requirement. This is especially the case when the requirement is phrased, as most law-ethic has tended to be, in negative terms: 'Thou shalt *not* . . .' Moral theologians have always maintained that a positive command is more difficult to obey than a negative one; and if this be true, the inclusive command to 'love one's neighbour' is the most difficult, not the least difficult. So much is this the case that some writers on ethics, such as Reinhold Niebuhr, have talked about 'the impossible possibility' of love in human action, although it is worth observing that in recent years Niebuhr himself has come to be a little more open to the chance that in some situations at least love *can* be effectively implemented in action.

No matter what may be our attitude on this point, we should recognize that in almost all significant Christian moral discussion today, both in the Roman Catholic Church and in Reformed churches, the emphasis is put on love and not on law. One might almost say that the most striking phenomenon of our times, so far as morality is concerned, is the re-discovery of love as the central criterion in ethical judgement. It is also the case, today, that in the same circles, with variations according to traditional modes of statement, man's ethical obligations are considered in the light of the actual, concrete, known situations in which he finds himself. This manner of discussing moral issues is practically universal; it does not matter whether those who take part are professed followers of 'situation ethics' – it is almost impossible to find anyone, even among the opponents of what they take that ethical line to affirm, who will not use, in actual practice, this approach. This was brought home to me recently when I attended a discussion of the principles which should govern the Christian as he deals with the problem of pre-marital sexual relations. One of those present was a vigorous defender of traditional 'Catholic principles' and expressed in no uncertain terms his contempt for the new 'permissive morality', as he called it. Yet when we came to consider particular aspects of the problem, he was the one to insist on love as the basis for all counselling and for all determination of 'right behaviour' and he was also the one to say, as if enunciating a new truth, 'Let us not forget, in handling these problems, that circumstances *always* alter cases.' He was a casuist, in the traditionalist sense; but his casuistry, as is always the case, was in effect nothing but the 'situation' approach applied to particular instances of behaviour.

Law has its place in moral matters. As the Bishop of Woolwich argued in his pamphlet *Christian Morality*, it can provide certain 'guide-lines' which will help us in forming our judgements; it will communicate to us the wisdom of our ancestors as they wrestled in their own day with moral issues. Indeed, in these ways law is indispensable to us, for without it we should be liable to succumb to a complete relativism. But if law is the funded wisdom of our ancestors, it also can provide us with splendid examples of their foolishness or their lack of understanding. They made mistakes, as we all do; much that is taken to be their profound wisdom is nothing of the sort. In any event, 'new occasions teach new duties', as the American poet James Russell Lowell wrote; he went on to say that 'time makes ancient good uncouth'. Both statements must be remembered. In new situations, men find themselves responsible in new ways; in those same new situations, much that was thought to be imperative is now seen to be impossible, perhaps even absurd, and often enough inadequately Christian. Whatever may be said positively about the place of law in ethical discussion, that place can never be the final one.

Some of us are convinced that what we need today is a courageous re-conception of the significance of Christian love in action, in the light of the present circumstances, and with due regard for the peculiar places in which people find themselves – situations, circumstances, and places which do not permit us to deliver ourselves of high-sounding principles that must be applied in detail, but make it necessary for us to relate the imperative to love, in all its intensity, to this or that particular issue as it is confronted by this or that particular man or woman. Anyone who has heard clerical discussion on such matters knows that all too often it appears to deal with moral decisions as if they were made in an imaginary world. Many moral theologians seem to live in remarkable isolation from the actual dilemmas which ordinary men and women, often devoutly Christian, must necessarily face every day of their lives.

Finally, as our fourth point, we come to what I have described as the requirement that Christians re-conceive their discipleship in terms of social action. By this I do not mean only engagement in large-scale activities; I mean the relational or social nature of *all* human life. No man is an individual, without such 'social appurtenance', as Baron von Hügel styled it; we have already tried to make this clear. What I am talking about is an awareness of, a sense of responsibility for, and a whole-hearted participation in relationships of all sorts, in which people actually do live; I am also talking about the requirement that we bear constantly in mind the truth that human beings are organic one to another and in consequence function in 'organizational' ways. Above all today as at no time in the past we have become conscious of this social patterning of human existence; the state of affairs as it actually is forces us to recognize that we can only be faithful to our common manhood by doing what we do and becoming what we are to become in terms of social consequences. This stress on human sociality should be welcomed by Christians, since it is in accordance with their deepest insight into man and their en-graced awareness of what constitutes him as distinctively human. The corollary of that insight and awareness, as well as the plain demands of our contemporary situation, should lead us to express in what I have styled 'social action' that which we know to be true. Otherwise there will be an intolerable dichotomy between what as Christians we profess to believe and what in concrete fact we are ready to do.

Much of the time, if not always, participation in what I have called 'social action' will be in non-religious contexts. It will be in 'secular' ways. But we have seen that there is no disjunction between the 'sacred' and the 'secular'; a Christian, above all, cannot think in that fashion if he has accepted the faith in the incarnate Lord. Hence participation in the affairs of the so-called 'secularized' society will be as much, perhaps even more, religious in the positive and right sense of that word as participation in the activities which are specific to churchly circles. The *whole world* is

God's; interest in it, entrance into its affairs, responsible action within it, at every point and place, is therefore the doing of God's work and obedience to God's will. Alas, it is sometimes true that particularized 'religious' activities are not this at all; they can amount to playing 'church-games', mostly harmless enough, but sometimes terribly wrong – and wrong because they divert our attention from the 'weightier matters' which God has laid upon us as our immediate human responsibility in the place where he has let us live, work, and act. There is always the danger that we shall permit ourselves comfortably to slip back into a 'churchiness' which can be disastrous. The danger is especially threatening for those of us who in one way or another are 'professionally' connected with ecclesiastical institutions – that is, for the clergy and for 'church-workers'.

I hope that it is plain enough that I do not decry the necessary concern of such persons with the institution, nor that I suppose there is no place for a genuine interest in the affairs of that institution. All I ask for, in this reconception of Christian discipleship in terms of social action, is that we retain our sense of proportion; put in another way, I urge that we have the right order of priorities. The ordinary Christian is much more likely to express his faith in his home, office, union, shop, school; in his business relations, his attitude to his neighbours, his family life, his concern for social, economic, political justice; much more likely to do it in such places and such ways than in acting as a sidesman (or usher, as they say in the United States) or attending meetings of church societies. To say this is to say the obvious. But what is needed is a thorough re-conception of ideas about Christian discipleship so that the obvious may become more *apparently* obvious. Unhappily this is by no means the case; and not enough has been said and done, even today, to convince either Christians or non-Christians that it is.

A rather vocal school of theologians have said that 'God is dead'. But many of us do not accept such an announcement. What is dead are *ideas* of God, *pictures* of him, which we should be glad to discard. If God is alive, vital, dynamic – working in his world through channels which most often are 'secular' – so is the Christian faith which finds its centre in his self-disclosure in Jesus Christ. But the Christian faith seems to many people today to be moribund. Why is this so? Largely because the way in which it has been stated, the notions associated with it, and much in the lives of those who profess it, have no contact with things as they are and as ordinary people know them to be. The world and society have changed. And the encouraging fact about some contemporary Christian thinking and planning, worshipping and praying, acting and working, is that it too is slowly changing. Every committed Christian today is called upon to play his part in this process, working for the re-conception of the faith and the life which that faith entails, so that the love of God, manifested in Jesus Christ, may be brought to bear upon contemporary existence in all its aspects. Only in this way can we be faithful to the trust which is ours.

Subject Index

Index of Names

(God, Jesus Christ, Holy Spirit, are not listed, since references to them appear on practically every page)